WAR DEPARTMENT

TECHNICAL MANUAL

ORDNANCE MAINTENANCE

BROWNING AUTOMATIC RIFLE, CAL. .30, ALL TYPES

March 1, 1942.

DISCLAIMER:

THIS MANUAL IS SOLD FOR HISTORIC RESEARCH PURPOSES ONLY, AS AN ENTERTAINMENT. IT CONTAINS OBSOLETE INFORMATION AND IS NOT INTENDED TO BE USED AS PART OF AN ACTUAL OPERATION OF MAINTENANCE TRAINING PROGRAM. NO BOOK CAN SUBSTITUTE FOR PROPER TRAINING BY AN AUTHORIZED INSTRUCTOR.

TECHNICAL MANUAL)   WAR DEPARTMENT,
    No. 9-1211   )   Washington, March 1, 1942.

ORDNANCE MAINTENANCE

BROWNING AUTOMATIC RIFLE, CAL..30, ALL TYPES

————◆————

**Prepared under direction of the
Chief of Ordnance**

————◆————

---

*This TM supersedes TR 1400-30 E, November 28, 1928.

Section I

INTRODUCTION

1.   SCOPE. - This manual is published for the information and guidance of ordnance maintenance personnel. It contains detailed instructions for inspection, disassembly, assembly, maintenance, and repair of the Browning Automatic Rifles, Cal. .30, M1918, M1918A1, and M1918A2 (figs. 1, 2, 3, and 4) supplementary to those in the Field Manuals prepared for the using arm.

2.   IDENTIFYING CHARACTERISTICS OF THE RIFLES. - The basic Browning Automatic Rifle pattern has been developed as four types; namely, Browning Automatic Rifle, Cal..30, M1918, M1918A1, M1918A2 and Browning Machine Rifle, Cal..30, M1922. Each type uses the same receiver. Some receivers, of early issue, are stamped "Browning Machine Rifle, Model of 1918" and others, "Browning Automatic Rifle, Model of 1918". The types may be distinguished by the following characteristics:

a.   Browning Automatic Rifle, Cal..30, M1918. - Smooth, slightly tapered barrel, 1-1/8 in. in diameter at the receiver. Smooth stock with butt swivel between grip and toe of butt. The butt plate is similar to the U.S. rifle, Cal..30, M1917, butt plate. Weight approximately 16 pounds.

b.   Browning Automatic Rifle, Cal..30, M1918A1. - Same barrel and stock as the M1918, with same location of butt swivel. The butt plate is hinged at its heel, mounting an outer butt plate. A bipod with spiked feet is attached to the gas cylinder just forward of the forearm. Weight, including bipod, is approximately 18.5 pounds.

c.   Browning Automatic Rifle, Cal..30, M1918A2. - May use same barrel as M1918 and M1918A1. Forearm is cut down around the barrel and shortened; a metal shield is inserted to protect recoil spring from heat. Bipod with skid type shoes is assembled to flash hider. Stock rest is mounted in recess in butt stock. Hinged butt plate mounting outer plate same as M1918A1, except that outer plate is shorter. Cyclic rate change mechanism housed in buffer and butt stock assembly.

d.   Browning Machine Rifle, Cal..30, M1922. - Finned barrel about 1-1/2 in. in diameter at the receiver. The butt swivel is secured to the left cheek of the stock. There is a wide groove around the stock to the rear of the comb in which a stock rest may be fitted. This stock rest and a bipod, which may be clamped around the barrel just forward of the forearm, are listed in SNL A-18, as accessories. This type rifle is now obsolete and no further reference to it is made in this manual.

3. BROWNING AUTOMATIC RIFLE, CAL..30, M1918A1. - The modification of the M1918 automatic rifle to the M1918A1 automatic rifle, includes the following points of change:

a. A bipod is mounted on the gas cylinder tube just forward of the forearm. This bipod consists of a split body which fits to gas cylinder tube and barrel and is clamped in place by four machine screws. Two hinged legs are attached to the body by pins held in place by cotter pins. The hinged leg is composed of a head and a tube in which the sliding leg is housed, prevented from sliding out of tube by a stop pin. To the sliding leg is welded a spiked foot, and to the left leg is attached a catch which engages the right leg when folded forward and holds both legs close to barrel. The sliding leg is locked by the tube clamp and thumb screw.

b. The forearm of the M1918A1 automatic rifle is shorter than that of the M1918, and cut away from the barrel for ventilation.

c. The butt plate of the M1918A1 automatic rifle is the same as that of the M1918, except that to it is welded a hinge lug mounting an outer butt plate. When in use, this outer plate is swung to a position parallel with top of butt stock and is locked in this position, or folded against the inner plate by a spring ball lock.

d. The M1918 and M1918A1 automatic rifles originally were furnished with a gun sling swivel link as part of the front swivel assembly. This link was subsequently removed, due to its tendency to wear out. (FSMWO A4-W3.)

e. There are now in use two types of gas cylinders. The older type has a solid head, while the newer type has a gas pressure relief vent running horizontally in the head and has slightly more piston clearance than the solid head type. For gaging these gas cylinders, refer to paragraph 38 c (2).

4. BROWNING AUTOMATIC RIFLE, CAL..30, M1918A2. - The modification of the M1918A1 automatic rifle to the M1918A2 automatic rifle includes the following points of change:

a. The flash hider of the M1918A1 automatic rifle is

3

replaced with a flash hider and integral bearing, upon which is mounted a bipod of different design from that pertaining to the M1918A1. This bipod has a tubular body which fits on the bearing of the flash hider and is held in position by a shoulder on the flash hider and a spring friction washer positioned between the rear of bipod body and the forward shoulder of the barrel, with spring bearing on bipod body.

b. The M1918A2 bipod consists of a body and two leg assemblies. The leg joints slide in vertical and horizontal slots in the bipod body and thus can be locked in extended or folded position (to rear) by thumb screws on which they pivot. The jointed leg tube houses a sliding leg with skid type shoe, which is prevented from sliding out of the tube by a floating key pivoted on the tube clamping thumb screw, and riding in a dead-end keyway in the sliding leg. The sliding leg is controlled by tube clamp and thumb screw.

c. The forearm of the M1918A2 automatic rifle is identical with that of the M1918A1, except that it contains a metal shield positioned in grooves in the wood of forearm to protect the recoil spring from barrel heat.

d. The rear sight assembly of the M1918A2, automatic rifle, is of different design from that of the M1918A1. The M1918A2 rear sight has both windage and elevation adjustment controlled by large knobs and click mechanism, while the M1918A1 rear sight is adjustable for elevation only and is without click mechanism. The base of the M1918A2 rear sight has a larger base set screw and hole than the corresponding base spring screw and screw hole of the M1918A1. This smaller screw hole has been modified to conform with that in the M1918A2 rear sight base in order that the larger screw might be common to both types (FSMWO A4-W2).

e. A right and left magazine guide have been added (to the M1918A2), fastened to the trigger guard body by machine screws staked in. These guides facilitate insertion of the magazine.

f. The outer butt plate of the M1918A2 rifle is shorter than that of the M1918A1 to obviate interference with shoulder when rifle is fired in the prone position.

g. The M1918A2 automatic rifle is equipped with a stock rest which fits into a bearing positioned in the butt stock and to which the butt swivel is attached. This stock rest is composed of a nut pinned to a stem which is retained in the bearing when positioned by a spring ball lock. The nut is threaded to take an elevating screw to which is riveted a spiked foot. The elevating screw is locked in position by a lock nut. The stock rest is not used except when the M1918A2 rifle is used as a substitute for the light machine gun in such units.

    h.   The M1918A2 automatic rifle is furnished with a cyclic rate mechanism housed in the butt stock, and a modified trigger guard mechanism. The purpose of the cyclic change mechanism is to furnish a reduced rate of automatic fire from 550 rounds per minute (normal cyclic rate) to 350 rounds per minute (slow cyclic rate). The most effective volume of fire of this weapon is from 120 to 150 rounds per minute. Parts of the M1918A1 automatic rifle affected by the cyclic rate mechanism are the sear, sear carrier, change lever spring, buffer, buffer tube, buffer nut, butt stock bolt, butt stock bolt washer, and butt stock. For description and functioning of the cyclic change mechanism, refer to FM 23-15, section on "Functioning".

RA FSD 2533

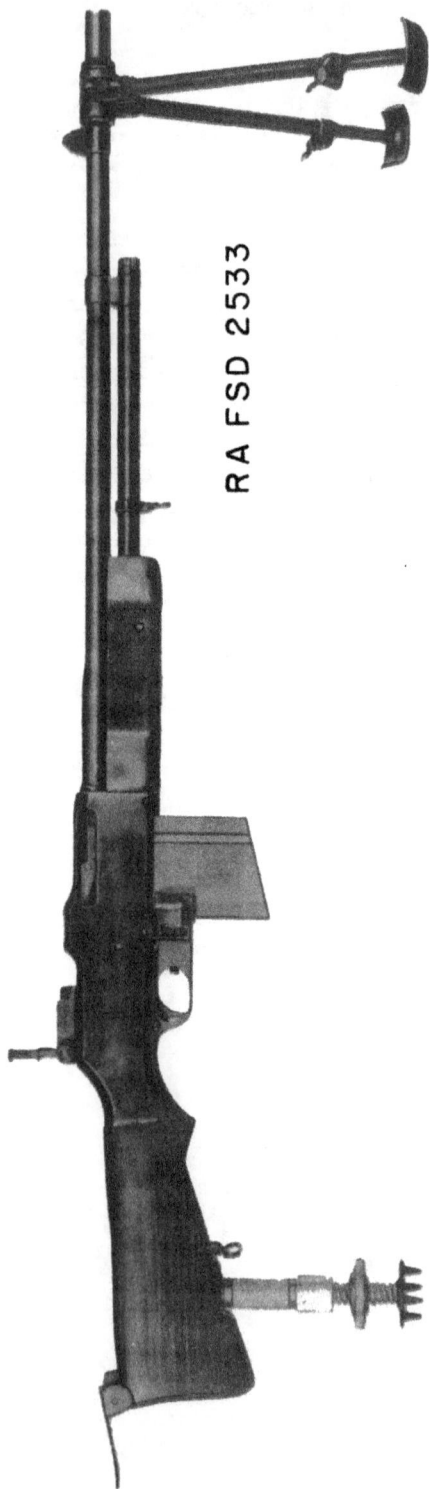

FIGURE 1 — BROWNING AUTOMATIC RIFLE, CAL. .30, M1918A2 - RIGHT SIDE VIEW

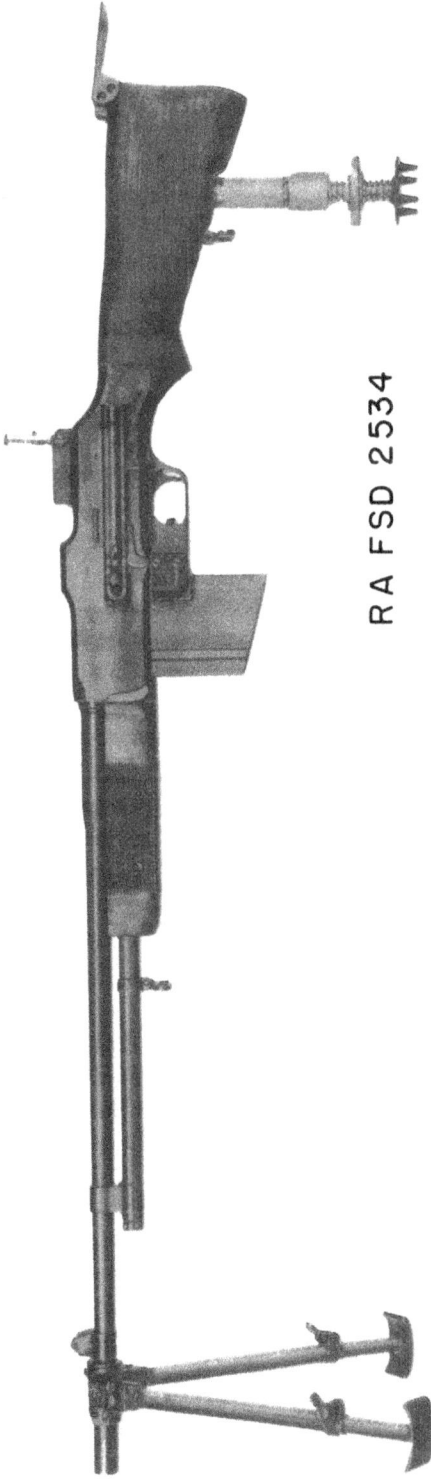

RA FSD 2534

FIGURE 2 — BROWNING AUTOMATIC RIFLE, CAL. .30, M1918A2 - LEFT SIDE VIEW

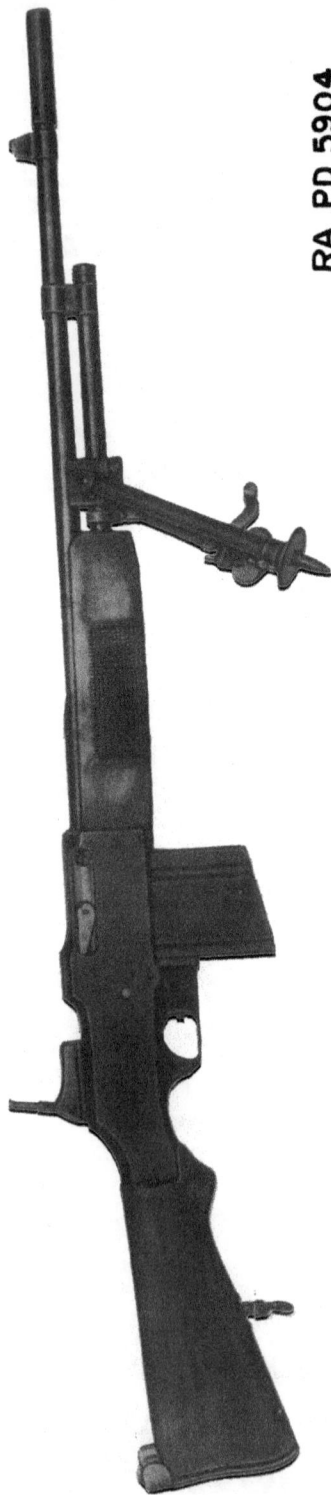

RA PD 5904

FIGURE 3 — BROWNING AUTOMATIC RIFLE, CAL. .30, M1918A1 - RIGHT SIDE VIEW

RA PD 4199

FIGURE 4 — BROWNING AUTOMATIC RIFLE, CAL. .30, M1918 - RIGHT SIDE VIEW

Section II

DISASSEMBLY AND ASSEMBLY

5. GENERAL. - a. Disassembly and assembly of the Browning automatic rifle as described in this technical manual is treated from the standpoint of a complete inspection of assemblies and parts subject to replacement or repair. Much of the disassembly described is unnecessary for a general or field inspection. Assemblies and parts disassembled from the rifle should be placed on a flat, clean surface and care exercised to prevent loss of

small pins, screws and like parts. Parts should be thoroughly
cleaned and oiled before reassembling, and gun lubricated where
necessary. For cleaning and lubrication refer to FM 23-15 and
FM 23-20, Section on "Care and Cleaning".

b. Disassembly and assembly of the rifle, as treated
herein, will, for convenience, comprise the dismounting and
mounting of groups in connection with the disassembly and assembly of the operating and trigger mechanism groups, necessary
for a general inspection, and in addition, the complete disassembly and assembly of the group assemblies for a complete inspection in their proper order.

6. DISMOUNTING OF GROUPS AND DISASSEMBLY OF OPERATING
GROUP. - a. Unscrew flash hider and remove bipod assembly and
friction washer (M1918A2). Remove stock rest (M1918A2) by
pulling out of bearing.

b. Remove bipod assembly (M1918A1) by filing off upsetting
of screws and removing screws from body, and body from gas cylinder tube.

c. Lay rifle on table, barrel down, pointing to left.
Cock the rifle. This must be done in order that the gas cylinder tube may clear the gas piston and gas cylinder tube bracket,
female. Turn gas cylinder tube retaining pin spring 180 degrees
in a clockwise direction and lift out gas cylinder tube retaining
pin. Remove gas cylinder tube and forearm by sliding forward.
Let slide forward easily by pressing trigger with thumb of right
hand and, at the same time, grasping slide with left hand so
middle and index fingers are astride gas piston.

d. Turn trigger guard retaining pin spring 90 degrees in
a clockwise direction and lift out pin. Lift out trigger guard
group (fig. 14). Remove recoil spring guide by pressing right
index finger on checkered surface of its head and turning it
until ends are clear of retaining shoulders (fig. 11).

e. Line up hammer pin holes on receiver and operating
handle by inserting point of recoil spring guide or dummy
cartridge in hole in operating handle with right hand, pressing
against hammer pin, and pushing operating handle backward with
left hand. The recoil spring guide will push hammer pin through
its hole in receiver as hammer pin registers with latter. Remove operating handle by pulling straight to rear. Remove
hammer pin. Push slide to rear and push hammer forward out of
its seat in slide and lift out of receiver. Remove slide by
pulling it forward out of receiver, being careful that bolt link
is pushed well down, allowing slide to clear. In removing

slide, take care to avoid striking gas piston or rings against gas cylinder tube bracket.

_f_. Force bolt guide out with left thumb or point of a bullet (fig. 11). Lift out bolt, bolt lock, and bolt link by pulling them slowly to rear end of receiver and up with right thumb and forefinger. Pull out firing pin from its way in bolt. Push out bolt link pin and remove bolt link. Do not remove bolt lock pin unless necessary as it is riveted (spun) in position. To remove, drive out from right side, using punch. Remove extractor by pressing point of a dummy cartridge against claw and exerting pressure upward and to front. Remove extractor spring.

7. TRIGGER MECHANISM, DISASSEMBLY (figs. 5 and 14). - _a_. Depress ejector lock with point of a dummy cartridge. Hold thumb in front of magazine catch spring to prevent it from flying out and then slide ejector out of its seat. Remove magazine catch spring. Remove magazine catch pin, lift out magazine catch and magazine release. Remove ejector lock and spring.

_b_. Insert trigger guard retaining pin spring (as tool) under sear spring above connector stop. Pry up, pressing against sear spring with thumb, and pull it out to rear. Push out trigger pin. The trigger pin must always be removed before sear pin in order that force of counterrecoil spring will always be on sear pin. Remove trigger and connector through top of trigger guard.

_c_. Push out sear pin with the recoil spring guide (as tool). Remove sear and sear release stop lever (M1918A2). Separate sear release stop lever from sear. Pry up on rear of sear carrier and lift out sear carrier and counterrecoil spring.

_d_. Remove change lever spring by prying bent end out of its seat, with rounded end of sear spring (as tool), and moving change lever from front to rear. When clear of change lever, push it out the rest of the way by pressing with thumb against base of sear release stop lever spring (M1918A2). (Change lever spring M1918 and M1918A1.) Pull out change lever.

_e_. To remove magazine guides, punch out staking and remove screws.

8. TRIGGER MECHANISM, ASSEMBLY. - _a_. Replace change lever. Insert ears of change lever spring in slots in trigger guard, sear release stop lever spring being up and to rear (M1918A2), push spring forward into place. Replace counterrecoil spring on counterrecoil spring guide (front of sear carrier). Insert counterrecoil spring guide into its seat. Brace forward end of trigger guard against a solid object, and with thumbs of right and left hands pressing on rear of sear

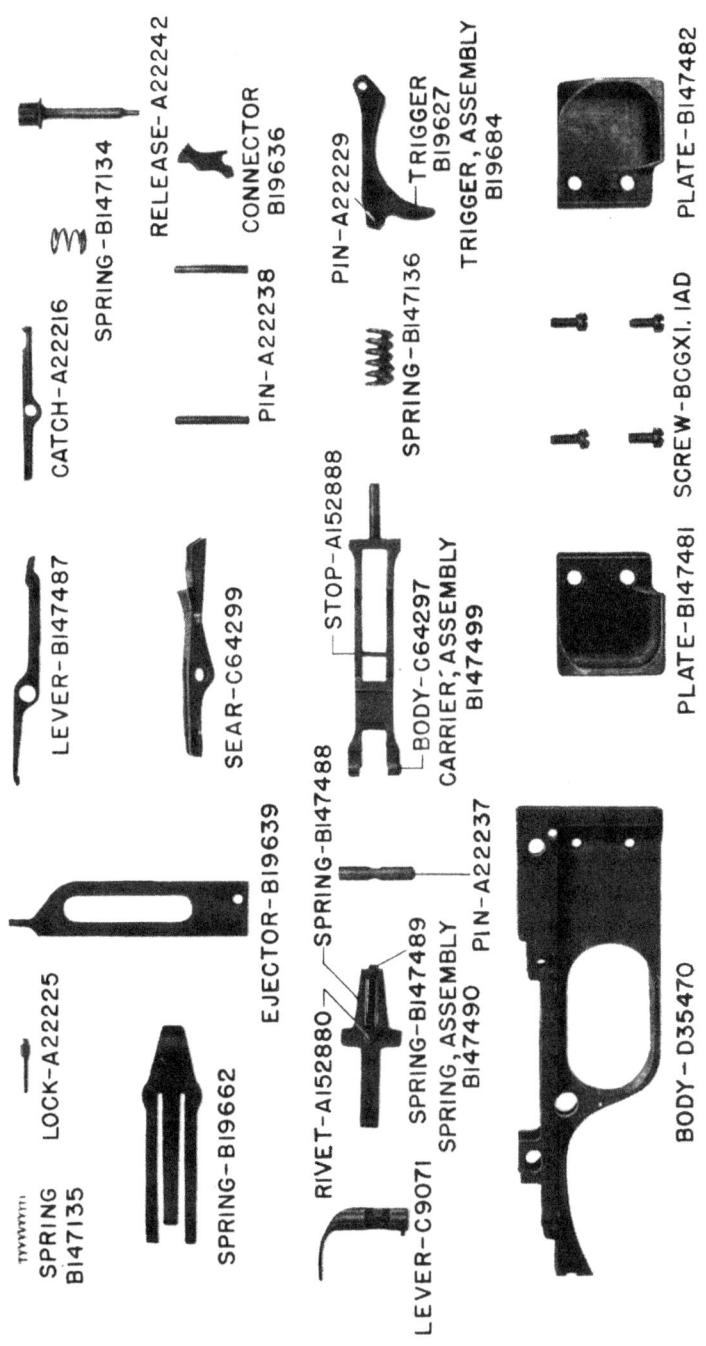

SPRING
B147135

LOCK-A22225

CATCH-A22216

SPRING-B147134

RELEASE-A22242

CONNECTOR
B19636

PIN-A22238

PIN-A22229

TRIGGER
B19627

TRIGGER, ASSEMBLY
B19684

PLATE-B147482

RA FSD 2541

LEVER-B147487

SEAR-C64299

SPRING-B147136

SCREW-BCGX1.1AD

SPRING-B19662

EJECTOR-B19639

STOP-A152888

BODY-C64297

CARRIER, ASSEMBLY
B147499

PLATE-B147481

LEVER-C9071

RIVET-A152880

SPRING-B147488

SPRING-B147489

SPRING, ASSEMBLY
B147490

PIN-A22237

BODY-D35470

FIGURE 5 — BROWNING AUTOMATIC RIFLE, CAL. .30, M1918A2 - TRIGGER GUARD GROUP - PARTS

13

carrier, push sear carrier forward until rear end is held by ears of change lever spring. Hold sear so sear nose is facing up and to rear. Insert short end of sear release stop lever (M1918A2) upward through slot in forward part of sear, taking care that notched end is down. Aline sear pin hole of sear release stop lever with sear pin hole in sear. Replace sear and sear release stop lever and force recoil spring guide through sufficiently, using recoil spring guide as lever, so as to aline holes in sear release stop lever, sear, sear carrier and trigger guard for sear pin. By slight pressure on recoil spring guide push sear carrier forward against counterrecoil spring, thus permitting sear pin to be seated easily in sear pin hole. The sear pin must always be replaced before trigger pin in order that force of counterrecoil spring will always be on sear pin. Replace trigger and trigger pin.

<u>b</u>. Holding connector so its head is in rear of connector stop, and toe is down and to rear, depress rear end of sear and drop connector into its place in trigger. Engage sides of sear spring in recesses and press down and forward on sear spring with thumb of right hand until front end of spring rests in depression stop. Take care to see that outside prongs of sear spring rest on their seat on sear and that middle prong rides freely in slot formed by walls of sear carrier. If middle prong rests on one of walls, instead of riding freely between them, trigger mechanism will not function when barrel is inclined below horizontal.

<u>c</u>. Replace magazine release, magazine catch, and magazine catch pin. Replace magazine catch spring. Insert ejector into recess and move it down until it is flush with magazine catch spring Insert ejector lock spring and lock into lock spring recess. Compress magazine catch spring in its seat and move ejector down until it is fully home and ejector lock is in its position.

<u>d</u>. After trigger mechanism has been assembled, turn change lever to forward position, and pull trigger. If connector will not rise, it is not in place correctly. It should rise and snap out from under sear. If connector will rise but does not raise sear, sear spring is weak and should be replaced.

<u>e</u>. To assemble magazine guides, replace screws, and restake.

9. ASSEMBLY OF OPERATING GROUP AND MOUNTING OF GROUPS. - <u>a</u>. Replace extractor spring in extractor. Replace extractor and spring in seat in bolt (fig. 21). Replace bolt link and

bolt link pin with shoulder of link against flat surface of bolt lock. Lift bolt lock and replace firing pin in bolt.

b. Lay rifle, barrel down, pointing to left so rifle is resting on barrel and rear sight base wings (fig. 11). With bolt mechanism held in a perpendicular position, insert it in receiver, forcing end of bolt under ends of bolt supports, and then press bolt mechanism down so as to lie flat in its place. Push bolt mechanism forward, swing bolt link down, then replace slide and push all the way back. With hammer resting between thumb and forefinger, lower and seat it properly in its seat in slide.

c. Push bolt lock fully into its locking recess and push slide forward. Gently insert hammer pin from right side in operating handle recess so that pin will enter hammer pin hole through operating handle recess connecting bolt link slide. Hammer pin is pushed through until it hits other side of the receiver, then pull slide gently to the rear, and at the same time, press on end of hammer pin with forefinger of right hand. (Hammer pin is protruding 1/4 in. from right side of receiver.) When hammer pin reaches hammer pin hole in receiver it will follow through hammer pin hole in receiver and will protrude 1/4 in. from left side of receiver. Take operating handle in the right hand between the thumb and forefinger and slide all the way forward in operating handle recess. With thumb of left hand push hammer pin into position as far as it will go and draw back mechanism.

d. Replace recoil spring and guide. With end of index finger on checkered end of recoil spring guide head, turn it until it is properly seated. Holding right thumb against forward end of receiver will facilitate this operation.

e. Replace trigger guard group and trigger guard retaining pin.

f. Cock the rifle. Slide gas cylinder tube and forearm to rear on gas piston, fitting lug to bracket dovetail (tapers to rear). Replace gas cylinder tube retaining pin.

g. To remount groups, replace flash hider friction washer on muzzle with spring forward, replace bipod assembly on flash hider and screw flash hider onto muzzle. Replace stock rest if necessary.

h. Replace bipod assembly (M1918A1) on gas cylinder tube, and replace screws, and restake heads, or replace with standard screws and upset the nose. Test rifle by hand operation and pulling of trigger.

10. FOREARM GROUP, DISASSEMBLY (fig. 6). - <u>a</u>. Slide forearm shield (M1918A2) to rear and remove. Unscrew forearm screws, long and short, and remove wood forearm from gas cylinder tube (screw is staked in escutcheon). The forearm escutcheon should never be removed from the forearm except for repair; to remove, insert screw and pull out. Unscrew bracket swivel screw which allows the removal of bracket swivel. Spring front swivel bracket off over gas cylinder tube. (Do not remove unless necessary.)

<u>b</u>. Before removing gas cylinder, note its setting carefully so it may be reassembled to same position. Then force out gas cylinder lock until its head clears notch in gas cylinder, which may then be unscrewed from gas cylinder tube. The gas cylinder lock may be completely removed from cylinder with a suitable drift, or by prying under head with combination tool.

11. FOREARM GROUP, ASSEMBLY. - Replace wood forearm on gas cylinder tube and insert the forearm screws, long and short. Slide forearm shield (M1918A2) into slots in wood, concave face up, aperture to rear. Spring front swivel bracket over gas cylinder tube and replace bracket swivel, fastening it in place with bracket swivel screw. All screws should be drawn up tight. Screw gas cylinder in gas cylinder tube to its proper setting and push in gas cylinder lock so its head engages notch in gas cylinder. Registration of gas port is indicated by circle marking on front of cylinder. When on small port, smallest circle is toward barrel, and in this position cylinder should be about one turn from shoulder. Unscrew one-third turn successively to register larger ports.

12. BUTT STOCK AND BUFFER GROUPS (M1918 AND M1918A1), DISASSEMBLY. - <u>a</u>. The butt stock bolt may be unscrewed by inserting a long screwdriver through the hole in the inner butt plate body after the outer butt plate body (M1918A1) has been raised and the butt plate trap has been opened. To remove bolt with combination tool, butt plate assembly must first be removed by unscrewing butt plate screws. As soon as butt stock bolt has been loosened, butt stock may be withdrawn to the rear.

<u>b</u>. To disassemble butt plate assembly (M1918A1 and M1918A2), unscrew set screw and remove lock spring and steel ball. The outer plate body must not be removed unless necessary for replacement as the hinge pin is staked in place. To remove, punch out staking and drive out pin. Unscrew and remove butt plate trap spring screw and spring (all types). Then drive out butt plate trap axis pin and remove butt plate trap.

c. Removal of the butt stock permits disassembling of
buffer mechanism. Unscrew buffer nut, using combination tool,
and remove to rear in order mentioned, buffer spring, four sets
of buffer friction cups and cones, and buffer. The buffer tube
is threaded into receiver and should never be removed except for
replacement. To remove, place receiver in vise with leather
jaws, and unscrew buffer tube with strap wrench.

13. BUTT STOCK AND BUFFER GROUPS (M1918 and M1918A1),
ASSEMBLY. - To assemble the butt stock and buffer mechanism,
reverse the method outlined in disassembly. Special attention
should be given to see that the buffer spring is always assembled
behind the buffer friction cups and cones, and the cones behind
their respective mating cups. There being no adjustment of the
buffer mechanism, the buffer nut should always be screwed up
tight when assembling. Be careful not to cross threads.

14. BUTT STOCK AND BUFFER AND ACTUATOR GROUPS (M1918A2),
DISASSEMBLY (figs. 7 and 8). - a. The stock retaining sleeve
may be unscrewed in a manner similar to that described for the
butt stock bolt in paragraph 12. Unscrew stock retaining sleeve
from actuator stop and remove butt stock from receiver, retaining sleeve lock washer from stock aperture and actuator
spring and actuator from rear of actuator tube and buffer cap
assembly.

b. Unscrew actuator tube and buffer cap assembly (cap
brazed to tube) from buffer tube, using combination tool. Remove buffer spring, four sets of cups and cones, and buffer head,
key and sear depressor from rear end of buffer tube. Remove key
and sear depressor from buffer head.

c. Buffer tube is threaded into receiver and should not
be removed except for replacement or repair. To remove, clamp
receiver in vise with leather jaws, and unscrew with strap
wrench. Remove buffer tube and qualifying shim. Place draw
mark on buffer tube and receiver for convenience when reassembling.

d. To disassemble the butt plate assembly, proceed as
explained in paragraph 12.

e. Remove stock rest bushing by removing screws and with-
drawing bushing from aperture in butt stock.

15. BUTT STOCK AND BUFFER AND ACTUATOR GROUPS (M1918A2),
ASSEMBLY. - a. To assemble the butt stock, buffer and actuator
groups, reverse the method outlined in disassembly. When assembling buffer tube to receiver, one of the eight grooves in
head of tube must lie centrally horizontal with top of receiver

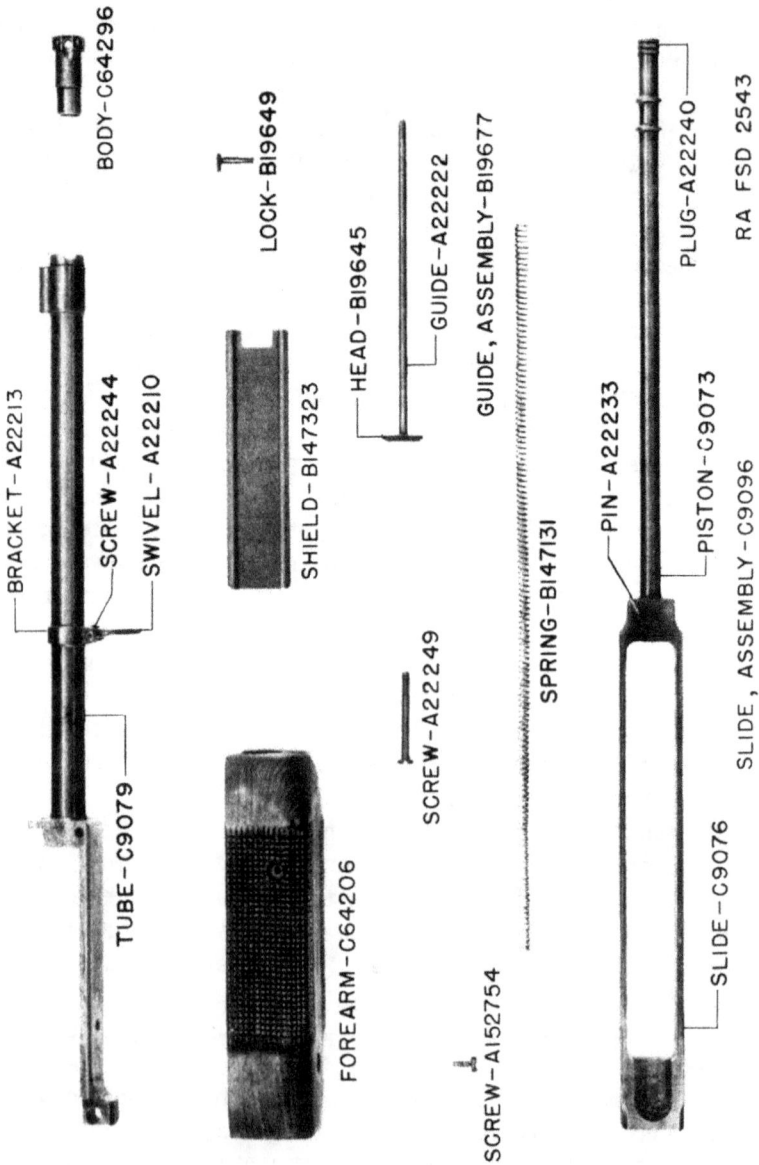

BODY–C64296

LOCK–B19649

BRACKET–A22213

SCREW–A22244

SWIVEL–A22210

SHIELD–B147323

HEAD–B19645

GUIDE–A22222

GUIDE, ASSEMBLY–B19677

TUBE–C9079

SCREW–A22249

SPRING–B147131

FOREARM–C64206

SCREW–A152754

PIN–A22233

PLUG–A22240

PISTON–C9073

SLIDE, ASSEMBLY–C9096

SLIDE–C9076

RA FSD 2543

FIGURE 6 — BROWNING AUTOMATIC RIFLE, CAL. .30, M1918A2 - GAS CYLINDER GROUP - PARTS

18

RELEASE-B147491

KEY-A152881

ACTUATOR-B147486

SHIM-A152884

SPRING-B147133

HEAD-B147492

SPRING-B147496

CAP-B147485

TUBE-B147493

SLEEVE-ASSEMBLY-C64298

TUBE-B147494

TUBE-B147495

CUP-A22218

CONE-A22217

RA FSD 2540

FIGURE 7 — BROWNING AUTOMATIC RIFLE, CAL. .30, M1918A2 - BUFFER GROUP - PARTS

19

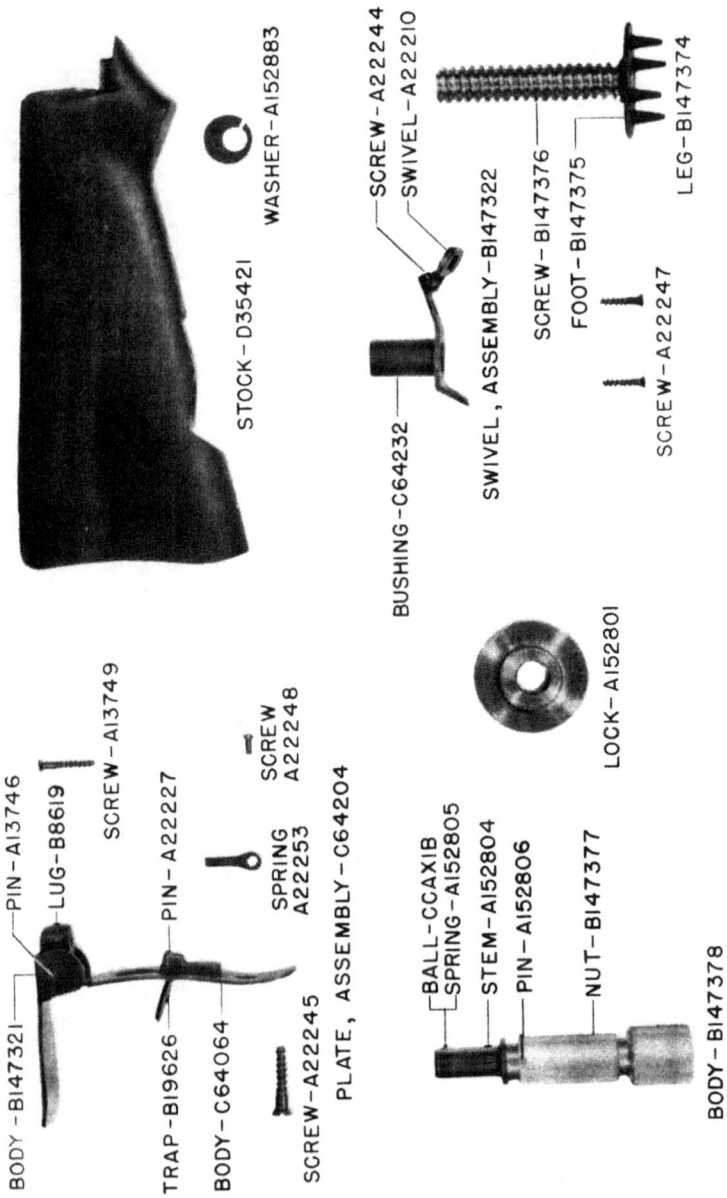

STOCK-D35421

WASHER-A152883

SCREW-A22244

SWIVEL-A22210

SWIVEL, ASSEMBLY-B147322

SCREW-B147376

FOOT-B147375

LEG-B147374

SCREW-A22247

BUSHING-C64232

RA FSD 2538

LOCK-A152801

PIN-A13746

LUG-B8619

SCREW-A13749

SCREW-A22227

PIN-A22227

SPRING A22253

SCREW A22248

BODY-B147321

TRAP-B19626

BODY-C64064

SCREW-A22245

PLATE, ASSEMBLY-C64204

BALL-CCAX1B

SPRING-A152805

STEM-A152804

PIN-A152806

NUT-B147377

BODY-B147378

FIGURE 8 — BROWNING AUTOMATIC RIFLE, CAL. .30, M1918A2 - BUTT STOCK GROUP - PARTS

20

to aline sear depressor head vertically in receiver, with nose
down. Buffer tube should be screwed up tight using qualifying
shim or shims, if necessary, to aline as explained. Be careful
not to cross threads.

b. Replace sear depressor in buffer head and replace key
so nose lies between positioning shoulders on sear release shank
with flat of notch to rear, to limit forward movement of sear
release.

c. Insert buffer head, cups and mating cones and buffer
spring in buffer tube in the order given, and replace buffer cap
and actuator tube assembly, screwing up firmly.

d. Replace butt stock retaining sleeve lock washer in
butt stock with prong to the rear and hole concentric with actuator tube hole. Assemble butt stock to receiver. Insert actuator in actuator tube, pointed end to rear, and replace actuator
spring, taking care that it seats evenly on rear shoulder of
actuator. Screw butt stock retaining sleeves in actuator tube
and draw up tight. Be careful not to cross threads.

e. Assemble butt plate assembly in reverse order to that
described for disassembly, and replace on butt stock.

f. Assemble butt swivel to stock rest bearing, replace
bearing in aperture in butt stock and replace screws.

16. RECEIVER GROUP, DISASSEMBLY. - a. To disassemble the
operating handle, press in on the operating handle plunger and
push out the operating handle plunger pin toward the countersunk
side of the plunger. The plunger and spring may then be removed.

b. The bolt guide spring may be lifted out of its seat
in the bolt guide with the rim of a cartridge. The guide and
spring may then be removed from the receiver.

c. To remove change lever stop and spring, depress spring
until clear of groove in change lever stop spring retaining pin,
shake pin from receiver, rotate spring down and push stop from
aperture in receiver.

17. RECEIVER GROUP, ASSEMBLY. - a. To assemble the operating handle, reverse the order of disassembly.

b. Insert the longer turned-over end of the bolt guide
spring in its hole inside of the receiver. Then replace the
bolt guide and hold it while the spring is pushed over until
the shorter turned-over end engages the groove in the bolt guide.

c. Replace change lever stop and spring in receiver and
secure with change lever stop spring retaining pin.

18. REMOVAL OF BARREL AND DISASSEMBLY OF BARREL GROUP. -
a. The barrel should never be removed until replacement is

necessary, and then only in a shop equipped with a suitable vise having leather jaws for holding the barrel and a special wrench and filler block for removing from the receiver. The special wrench and filler block for the Browning automatic rifle are provided for use in ordnance repair shops. Before removing barrel, remove from receiver the gas operating, firing and trigger mechanisms.

b. When necessary to remove barrel, using ordinary e-quipment, place front of receiver in vise with leather jaws, first wedging hard wood block between inside faces of receiver walls to prevent springing of receiver. Close vise just tight enough to hold receiver firmly. Uncorroded barrels should re-move easily with combination tool. If necessary, use strap wrench, or if barrel is to be scrapped, use pipe wrench. Fit wrench on barrel one inch from receiver and exert steady down pull (right hand thread).

c. The components attached to the barrel should never be removed except when replacements are necessary or for purposes of salvaging. To disassemble components, unscrew the flash hider with the combination tool. Drive out the front sight key pin, drive the front sight base off to the front, and remove the front sight key. The gas cylinder tube bracket may then be driven off to the front after the pin has been driven out.

19. ASSEMBLY OF BARREL GROUP AND REPLACEMENT OF BARREL. - a. Assemble parts in the reverse order to disassembly.

b. When replacing the barrel, always be sure that it is tight enough in the receiver never to work loose. Screw the barrel into the receiver until the draw line matches that of the receiver. Then assemble the gas cylinder tube to see if the gas cylinder tube bracket on the barrel lines up properly with the receiver so gas cylinder tube rear tang slides easily into its aperture in receiver. If it does not, the barrel should be turned very slightly until the alinement is correct. If barrel draw mark will not aline with draw mark on receiver, insert brass shim. When assembled, extractor cut in rear face of barrel should be checked for position. For assembling new barrel, refer to paragraph 77.

20. BIPOD ASSEMBLY (M1918A1), DISASSEMBLY. - a. Withdraw cotter pins from rod end pins, withdraw pins from body and re-move (right and left) hinged leg assemblies.

b. Unscrew thumb screws and position sliding leg in tube so stop pin registers with hole in hinged leg tube. Drive out stop pin and withdraw sliding leg assembly. Foot is welded to

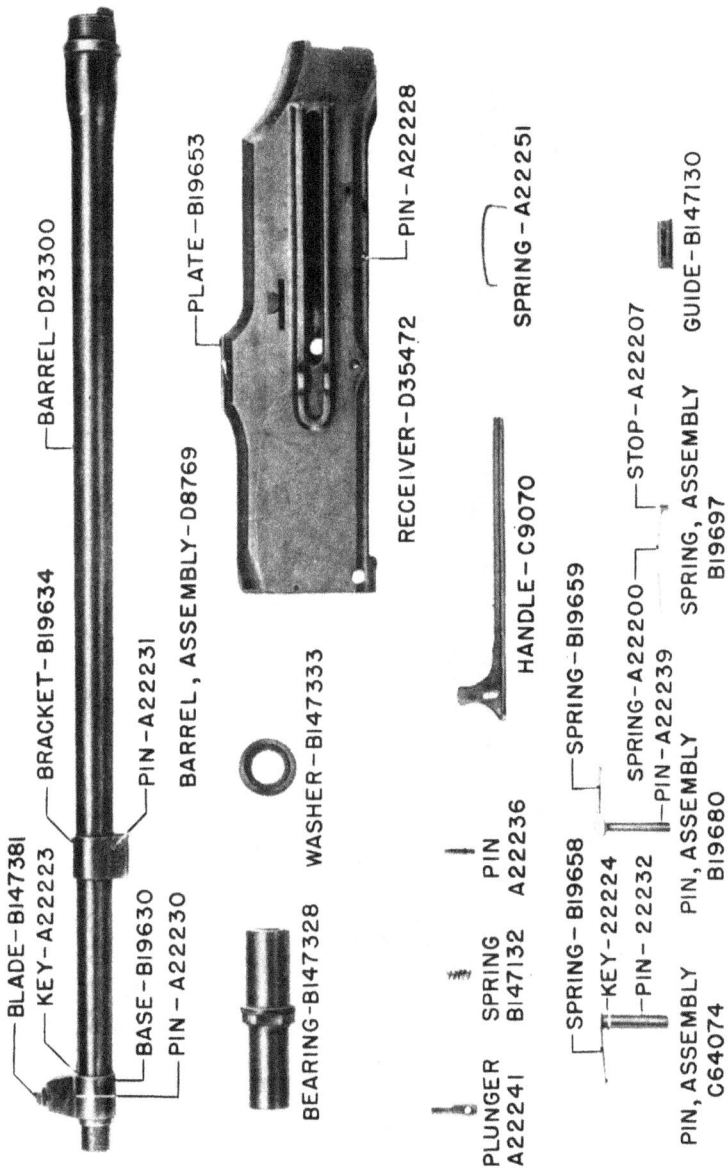

BARREL—D23300

BLADE—B147381

KEY—A22223

BRACKET—B19634

PIN—A22231

PLATE—B19653

BASE—B19630

PIN—A22230

BARREL, ASSEMBLY—D8769

PIN—A22228

RECEIVER—D35472

SPRING—A22251

BEARING—B147328

WASHER—B147333

HANDLE—C9070

STOP—A22207

GUIDE—B147130

PLUNGER
A22241

SPRING
B147132

PIN
A22236

SPRING—B19658

SPRING—B19659

SPRING—A22200

SPRING, ASSEMBLY
B19697

KEY—22224

SPRING—A22239

PIN—22232

PIN—A22239

PIN, ASSEMBLY
C64074

PIN, ASSEMBLY
B19680

RA FSD 2542

FIGURE 9 — BROWNING AUTOMATIC RIFLE, CAL. .30, M1918A2 - RECEIVER AND BARREL GROUP - PARTS

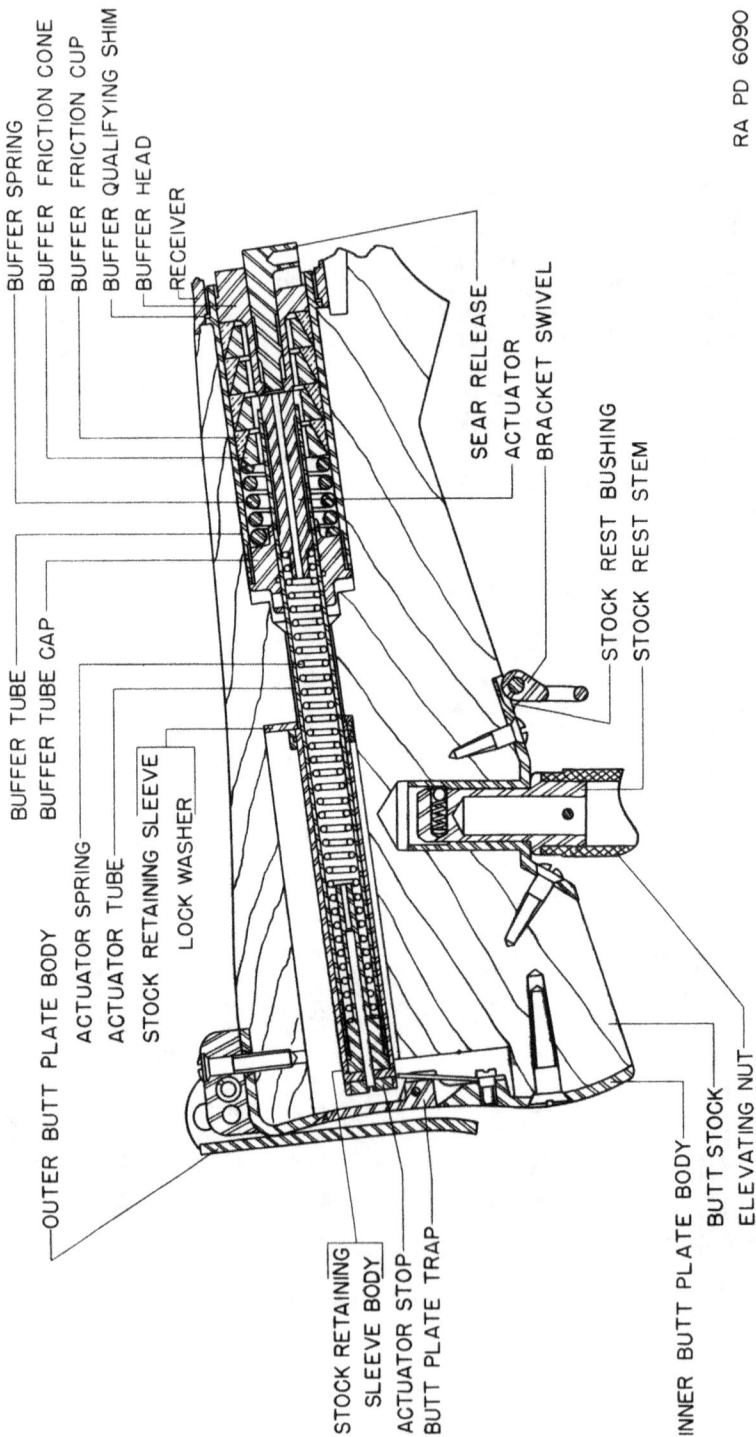

BUFFER SPRING
BUFFER FRICTION CONE
BUFFER FRICTION CUP
BUFFER QUALIFYING SHIM
BUFFER HEAD
RECEIVER

SEAR RELEASE
ACTUATOR
BRACKET SWIVEL

STOCK REST BUSHING
STOCK REST STEM

BUFFER TUBE
BUFFER TUBE CAP

ACTUATOR SPRING
ACTUATOR TUBE
STOCK RETAINING SLEEVE
LOCK WASHER

OUTER BUTT PLATE BODY

STOCK RETAINING
SLEEVE BODY
ACTUATOR STOP
BUTT PLATE TRAP

INNER BUTT PLATE BODY
BUTT STOCK
ELEVATING NUT

RA PD 6090

FIGURE 10 — BROWNING AUTOMATIC RIFLE, CAL. .30, M1918A2 - BUTT STOCK GROUP -
SECTIONAL VIEW - RIGHT SIDE

24

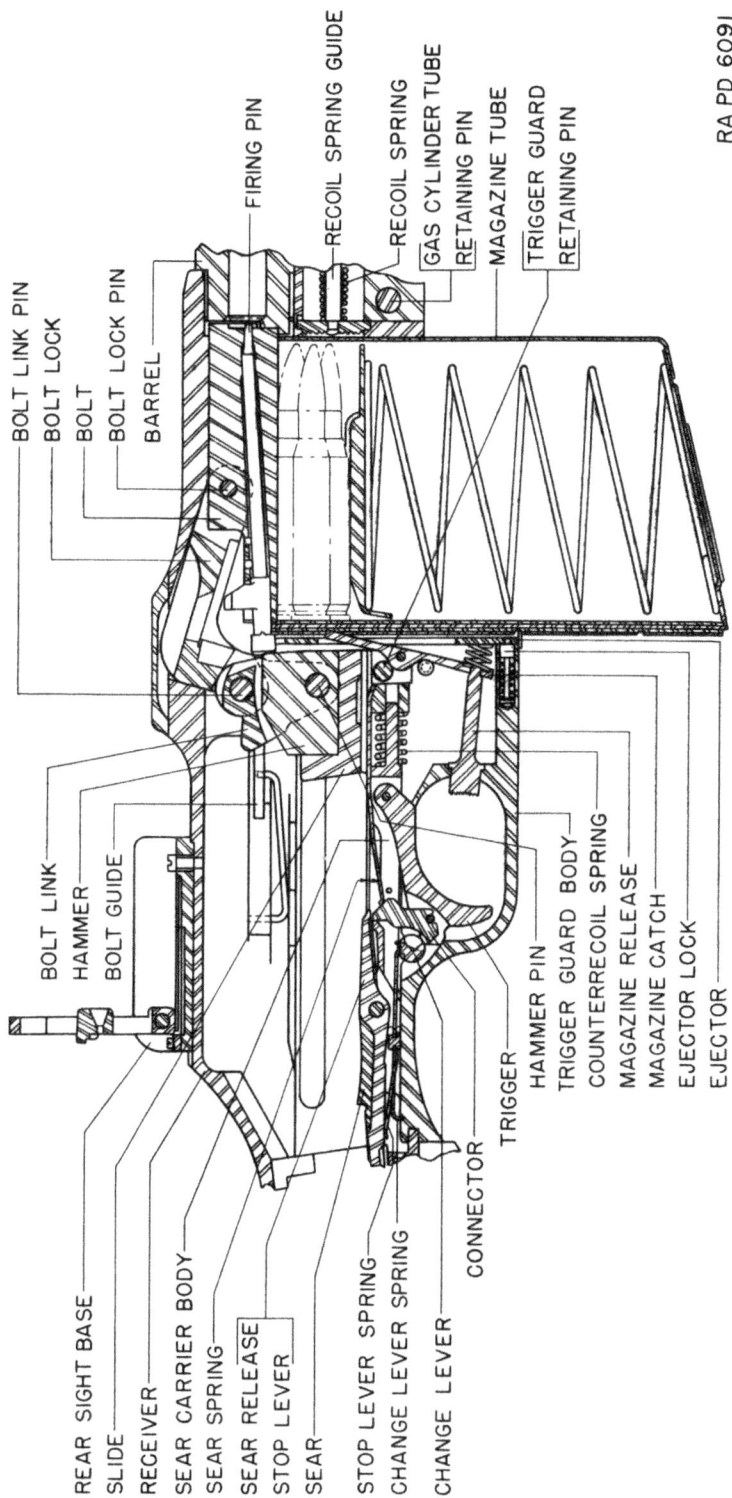

BOLT LINK PIN
BOLT LOCK
BOLT
BOLT LOCK PIN
BARREL

FIRING PIN
RECOIL SPRING GUIDE
RECOIL SPRING
GAS CYLINDER TUBE
RETAINING PIN
MAGAZINE TUBE
TRIGGER GUARD
RETAINING PIN

RA PD 6091

BOLT LINK
HAMMER
BOLT GUIDE

REAR SIGHT BASE
SLIDE
RECEIVER
SEAR CARRIER BODY
SEAR SPRING
SEAR RELEASE
STOP LEVER
SEAR

STOP LEVER SPRING
CHANGE LEVER SPRING
CHANGE LEVER

CONNECTOR
TRIGGER
HAMMER PIN
TRIGGER GUARD BODY
COUNTERRECOIL SPRING
MAGAZINE RELEASE
MAGAZINE CATCH
EJECTOR LOCK
EJECTOR

FIGURE 11 — BROWNING AUTOMATIC RIFLE, CAL. .30, M1918A2 - RECEIVER GROUP - SECTIONAL VIEW - RIGHT SIDE

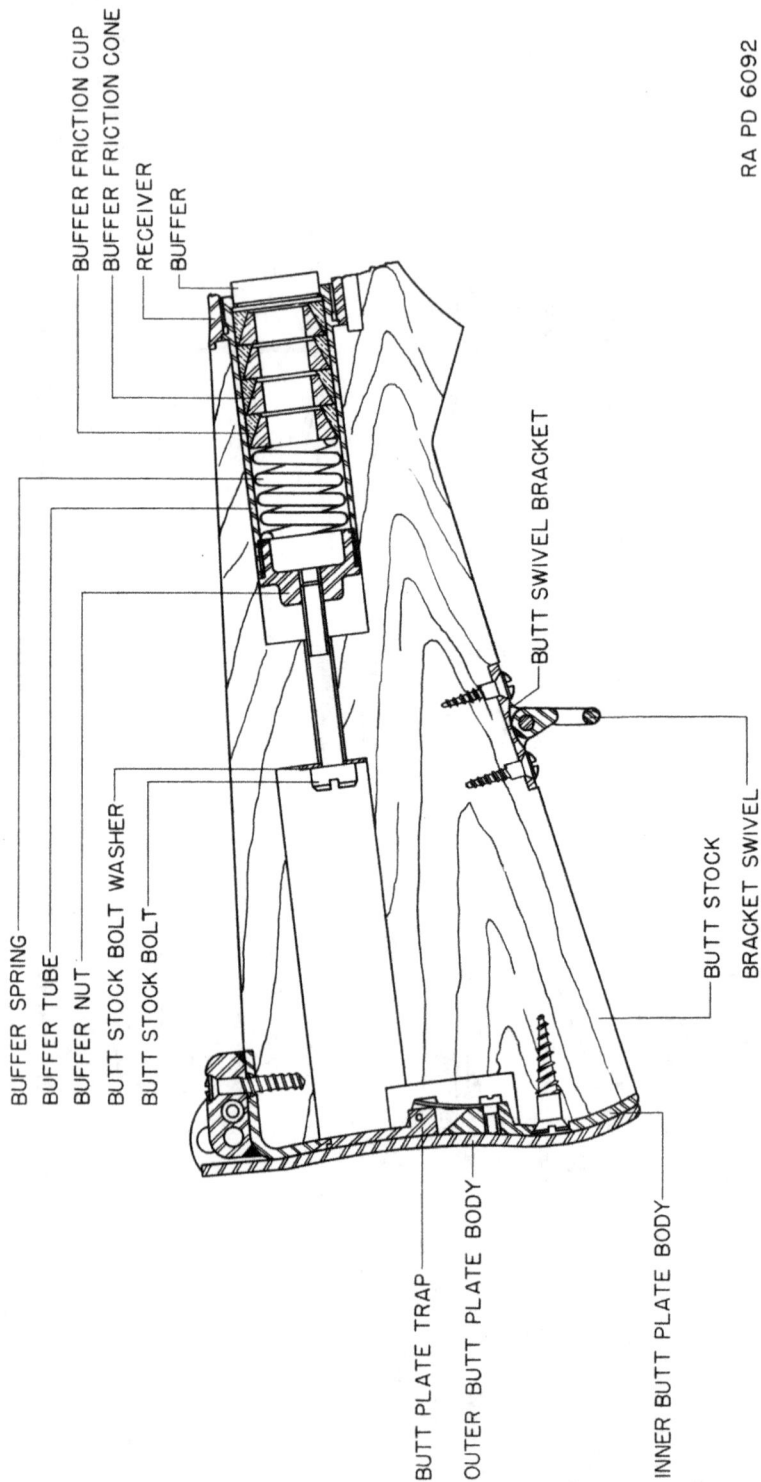

BUFFER FRICTION CUP
BUFFER FRICTION CONE
RECEIVER
BUFFER

BUFFER SPRING
BUFFER TUBE
BUFFER NUT
BUTT STOCK BOLT WASHER
BUTT STOCK BOLT

BUTT SWIVEL BRACKET

BUTT STOCK
BRACKET SWIVEL

BUTT PLATE TRAP
OUTER BUTT PLATE BODY

INNER BUTT PLATE BODY

RA PD 6092

FIGURE 12—BROWNING AUTOMATIC RIFLE, CAL. .30, M1918A1 - BUTT STOCK GROUP - SECTIONAL VIEW - RIGHT SIDE

26

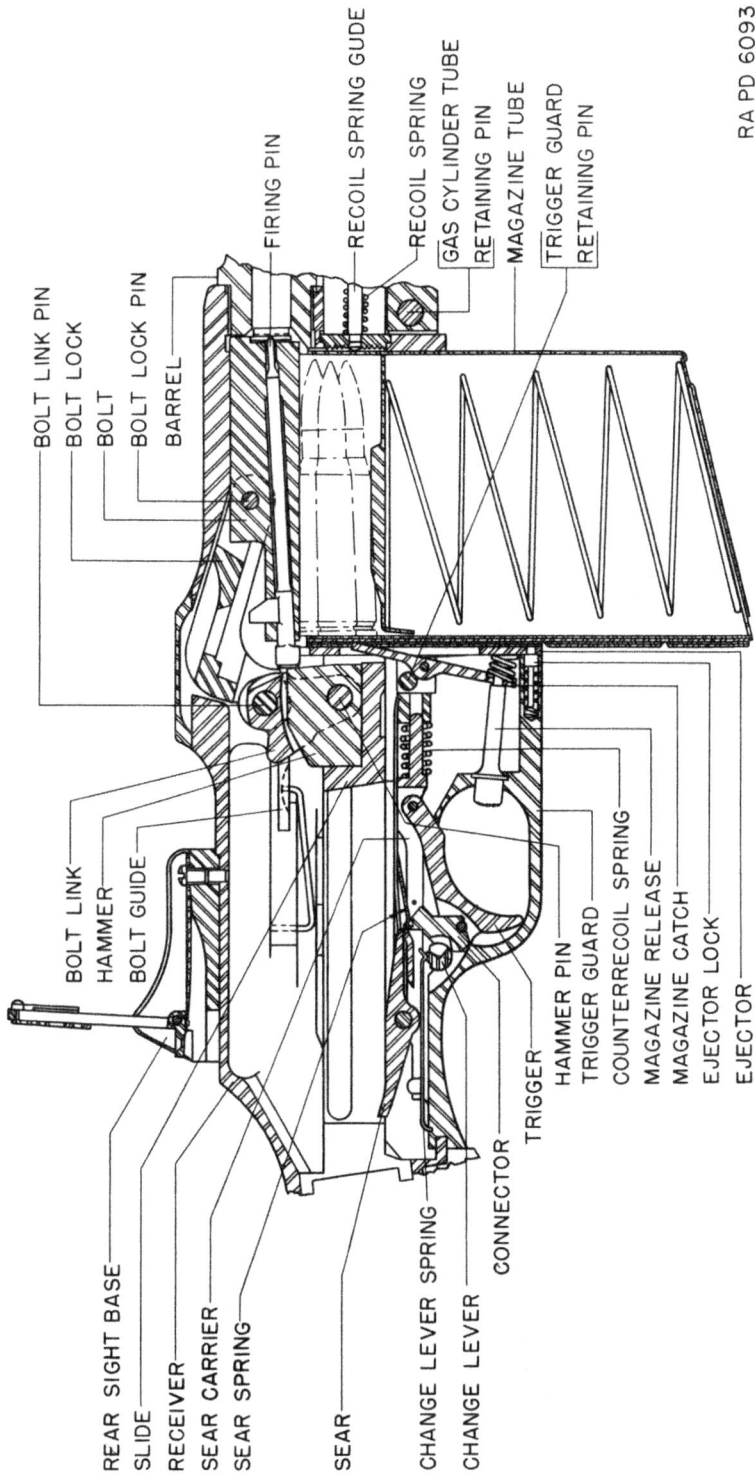

BOLT LINK PIN
BOLT LOCK
BOLT
BOLT LOCK PIN
BARREL

FIRING PIN
RECOIL SPRING GUDE
RECOIL SPRING
GAS CYLINDER TUBE
RETAINING PIN
MAGAZINE TUBE
TRIGGER GUARD
RETAINING PIN

BOLT LINK
HAMMER
BOLT GUIDE

HAMMER PIN
TRIGGER GUARD
COUNTERRECOIL SPRING
MAGAZINE RELEASE
MAGAZINE CATCH
EJECTOR LOCK
EJECTOR

REAR SIGHT BASE
SLIDE
RECEIVER
SEAR CARRIER
SEAR SPRING

SEAR

CHANGE LEVER SPRING
CHANGE LEVER
CONNECTOR
TRIGGER

RA PD 6093

FIGURE 13 — BROWNING AUTOMATIC RIFLE, CAL. .30, M1918A1 - RECEIVER GROUP - SECTIONAL VIEW - RIGHT SIDE

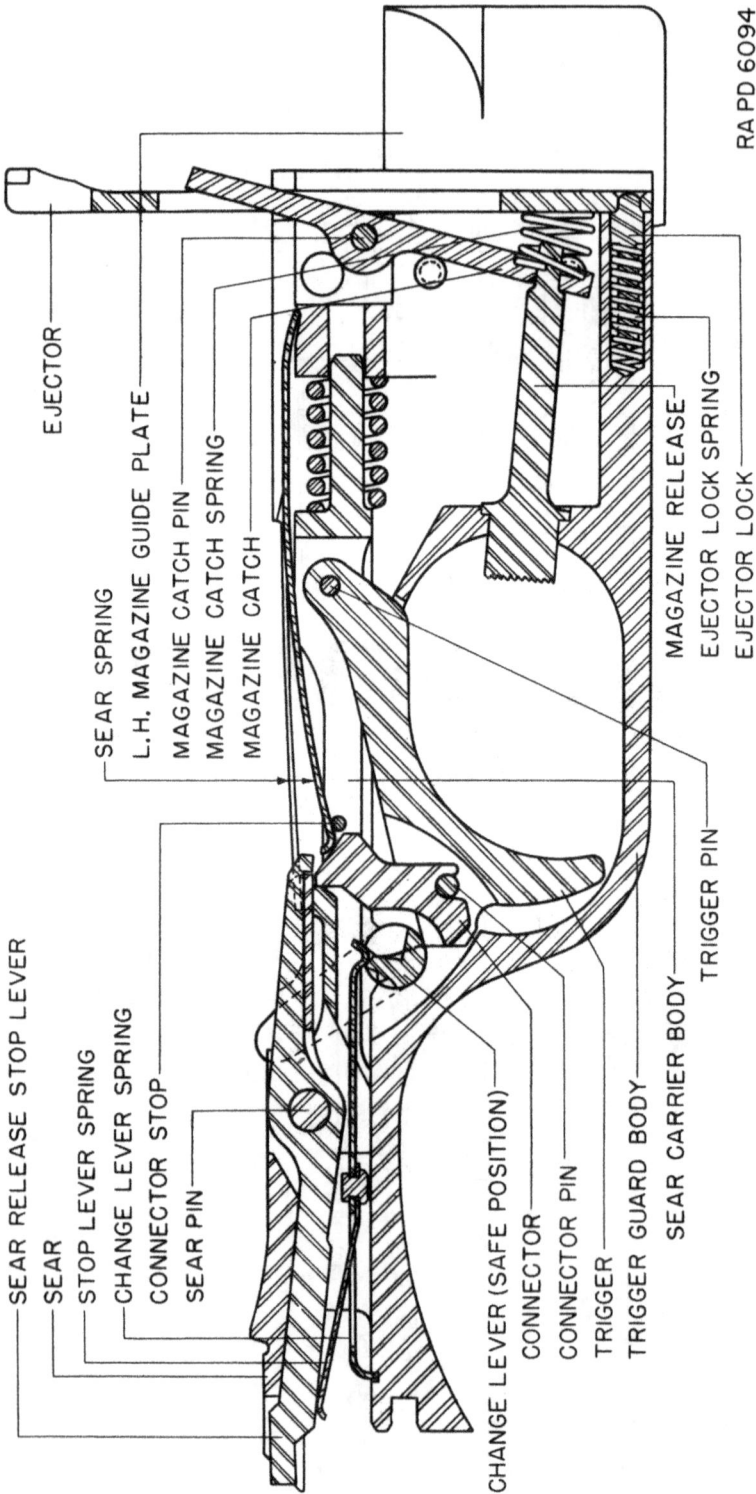

EJECTOR

SEAR SPRING
L.H. MAGAZINE GUIDE PLATE
MAGAZINE CATCH PIN
MAGAZINE CATCH SPRING
MAGAZINE CATCH

SEAR RELEASE STOP LEVER
SEAR
STOP LEVER SPRING
CHANGE LEVER SPRING
CONNECTOR STOP
SEAR PIN

CHANGE LEVER (SAFE POSITION)
CONNECTOR
CONNECTOR PIN
TRIGGER
TRIGGER GUARD BODY
SEAR CARRIER BODY

TRIGGER PIN

MAGAZINE RELEASE
EJECTOR LOCK SPRING
EJECTOR LOCK

RA PD 6094

FIGURE 14 — BROWNING AUTOMATIC RIFLE, CAL. .30, M1918A2 - TRIGGER GUARD GROUP - SECTIONAL VIEW - RIGHT SIDE

28

sliding leg, hinted leg tube to hinge, and clamp to hinged leg tube.

21. BIPOD ASSEMBLY (M1918A1), ASSEMBLY. - a. Replace sliding leg assembly in tube of hinged leg. Register stop pin holes in sliding leg and tube and insert stop pin. Replace thumb screws in clamp.

b. Replace hinged legs in body with thumb screws to rear, and replace rod end pins and cotter pins. Split cotter pins and bend snugly around rod end pins.

22. BIPOD ASSEMBLY (M1918A2), DISASSEMBLY (fig. 15). - a. Unscrew bipod leg thumb screws (upper) and remove right and left bipod leg assemblies from bipod body.

b. Unscrew bipod thumb screws (lower), remove bipod clamp leg keys, and remove bipod sliding legs from bipod leg tubes.

23. BIPOD ASSEMBLY (M1918A2), ASSEMBLY. - a. Replace bipod sliding leg assemblies in bipod leg tube. Replace two bipod clamp leg keys in their slots on right and left bipod sliding legs. Aline U-shaped opening of bipod clamp leg keys with holes in bipod leg clamps and replace bipod leg thumb screws (lower).

b. Replace bipod leg tubes in bipod body so unthreaded holes of bipod leg clamps are facing outward, and replace two bipod body thumb screws (upper).

24. STOCK REST GROUP (M1918A2), DISASSEMBLY AND ASSEMBLY. - a. Unscrew stock rest body and nut lock from elevating leg assembly. Do not disassemble further unless necessary. Elevating nut is pinned to stem (pin riveted) to comprise body assembly. To remove stem from nut, file riveting from one end of pin and punch out pin.

b. Elevating screw is riveted to foot to comprise elevating leg assembly. To remove foot, punch aluminum screw out of steel foot.

c. Ball lock and spring are staked in aperture. To remove, drill out staking with a blunt nosed drill.

d. To assemble, reverse procedure of disassembly, riveting pin and staking locking ball in apertures, and riveting screw in foot.

25. REAR SIGHT GROUP (M1918 AND M1918A1), DISASSEMBLY AND ASSEMBLY. - a. The rear sight is to be removed and disassembled only when a replacement of parts is necessary.

b. Unscrew the rear sight axis screw and nut and remove the rear sight leaf. The rear sight base spring may then be removed from the base, after screw has been removed.

c. Remove the rear sight base spring screw and drive the rear sight base out to the rear, using block of hard wood.

d. Unscrew the rear sight slide stop screw which will allow the slide to be withdrawn from the leaf. With a small drift, drive out the rear sight slide catch axis pin and take off the rear sight slide catch and spring.

e. To assemble the rear sight group, reverse the order of procedure given for disassembly.

26. REAR SIGHT GROUP (M1918A2), DISASSEMBLY AND ASSEMBLY (fig. 16). - a. Drive out windage knob pin from windage knob and remove knob from windage screw. Remove click plunger and spring from knob.

b. Unscrew windage screw to left and remove leaf assembly, remove base set screw and drive out base spring to rear. Remove windage scale screws from base and remove scale.

c. Drive base out of receiver to rear, using block of hard wood. Do not remove base unless necessary.

d. Drive out elevating screw knob pin from knob and remove knob from screw. Remove click plunger and spring from knob. Drive out elevating screw retaining pin and remove screw from leaf by unscrewing and removing from top. Remove slide from top front of leaf.

e. To assemble the rear sight group, reverse the order of procedure given for disassembly.

27. MAGAZINE, DISASSEMBLY AND ASSEMBLY (fig. 17). - a. Raise the rear end of magazine base until indentations on it are clear, then slide it to rear. The magazine follower and spring will then fall out.

b. Magazine is assembled in reverse order.

28. TO REMOVE AND REPLACE EXTRACTOR WITHOUT DISASSEMBLING. - a. Removal of extractor. - Draw operating mechanism to rear and insert an empty cartridge case between bolt and chamber, exposing extractor. Lay rifle on its side so ejection opening is up. With forefinger of left hand, force out claw of extractor, then place point of cartridge behind extractor shoulder and pry it forward until extractor is free of the recess. Remove extractor spring.

b. Replacement of extractor. - Insert short end of extractor spring in hole in shank of extractor so long end of spring is along slot in extractor. Insert extractor and spring in end of bolt and push them into position. Retract bolt and allow empty cartridge case to fall out of bottom of receiver.

29. TO REMOVE FIRING PIN WITHOUT DISASSEMBLING (fig. 17). -

a. <u>Removal of firing pin</u>. - Lay rifle on table, barrel down, muzzle to front. Remove trigger mechanism. Place rim of dummy cartridge under bolt guide, pull operating handle to rear and hold mechanism back. Steady cartridge with thumb and forefinger of right hand. It may be necessary to exert slight downward pressure on nose of cartridge in order to pull bolt guide out far enough to free bolt. Push down on bolt link, causing bolt to break at bolt lock pin. Allow mechanism to go forward until it stops. Remove firing pin.

b. <u>Replacement of firing pin</u>. - Insert firing pin in its aperture in bolt. Pull operating handle to rear again and push bolt into position.

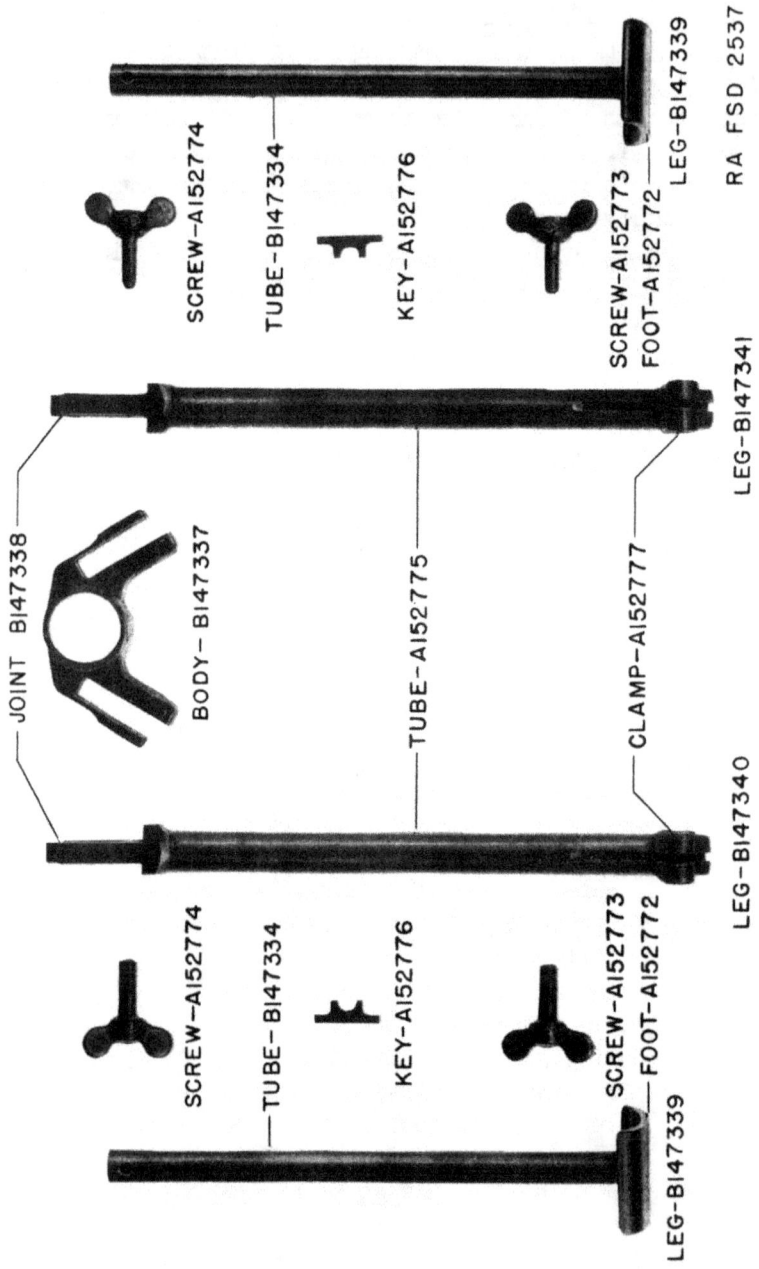

SCREW-A152774

TUBE-B147334

KEY-A152776

SCREW-A152773
FOOT-A152772

LEG-B147339

RA FSD 2537

JOINT B147338

BODY-B147337

TUBE-A152775

CLAMP-A152777

LEG-B147341

LEG-B147340

SCREW-A152774

TUBE-B147334

KEY-A152776

SCREW-A152773
FOOT-A152772

LEG-B147339

FIGURE 15 — BROWNING AUTOMATIC RIFLE, CAL. .30, M1918A2 -
BIPOD GROUP - PARTS

32

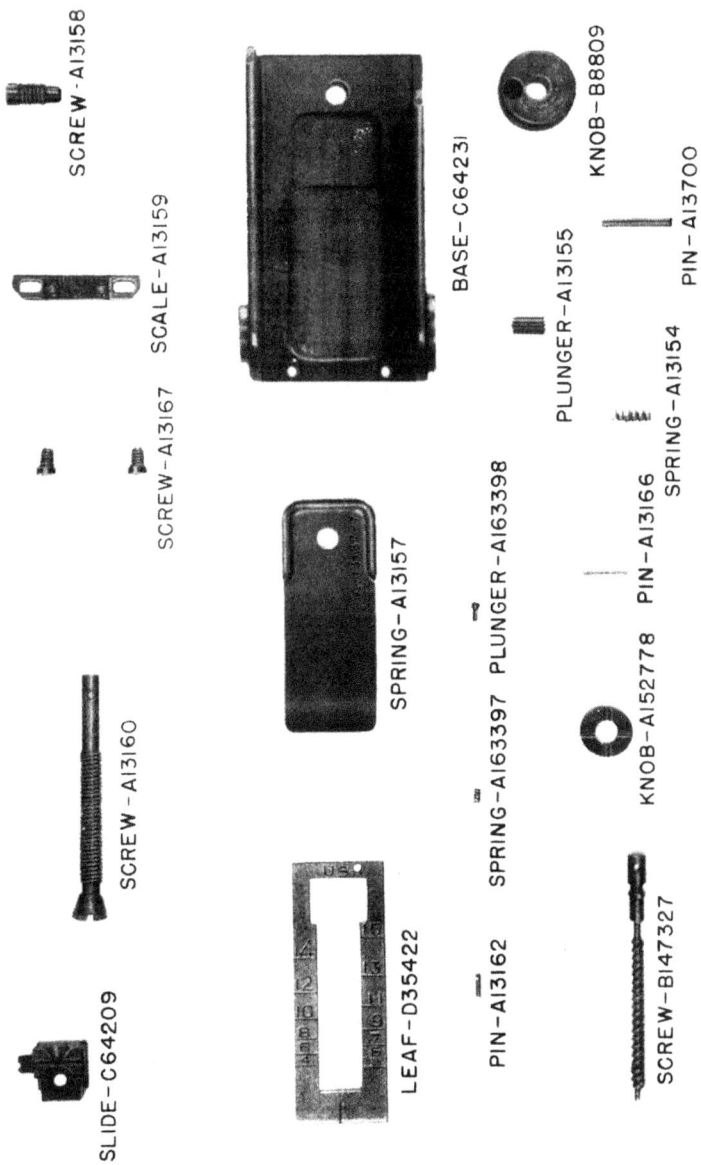

SCREW - A13158

SCALE - A13159

SCREW - A13167

SCREW - A13160

SLIDE - C64209

PIN - A13162

LEAF - D35422

SPRING - A163397

SPRING - A163398

PLUNGER - A163398

SPRING - A13157

KNOB - A152778

SCREW - B147327

BASE - C64231

PLUNGER - A13155

SPRING - A13154

PIN - A13166

KNOB - B8809

PIN - A13700

RA FSD 2539

FIGURE 16 — BROWNING AUTOMATIC RIFLE, CAL. .30, M1918A2 - REAR SIGHT GROUP - PARTS

33

TUBE-C9078

FOLLOWER-BI9641

BASE-BI963I

HAMMER-BI9643

PIN-A22234

RA FSD 2585

SPRING-C9077

SPRING-A22202

EXTRACTOR-C9090

PIN-BI9652

LOCK-C9072

PIN-A22226

BOLT-C9068

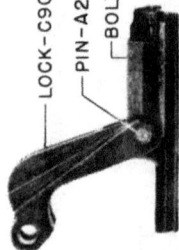

BOLT, ASSEMBLY-BI9695

PIN-A22235

LINK-BI9646

FIGURE 17 — BROWNING AUTOMATIC RIFLE, CAL. .30, M1918, M1918A1, M1918A2 -
BOLT AND MAGAZINE GROUP - PARTS

34

Section III

TOOLS FOR INSPECTION

30. GENERAL. - Tools for inspection, maintenance and repair, including general and special tools, are listed in SNL A-35 and SNL G-72, and carried on the small arms repair truck. The combination tool, gas cylinder cleaning tool, and barrel reflector are issued as organization equipment for these rifles.

31. USE OF TOOLS. - <u>a</u>. Gage, gas cylinder, (B.A.R.) (A77204). - Used to determine wear of gas cylinder. (Refer to par. 38 <u>c</u> (2).)

<u>b</u>. Gages, headspace, 1.940 in. (C7719A), 1.946 in. (C7719G), 1.950 in. (C7719M). - Used to check headspace and wear in chamber.

<u>c</u>. Gage, piston, (B.A.R.) (A77201). - Used to determine wear of the piston.

<u>d</u>. Gage, depth, micrometer (grad. in 1/1000 in.). - Used in conjunction with 1.940-in. headspace gage to determine excessive depth of barrel chamber.

<u>e</u>. Gage, breech bore, (C3940). - Used to determine the distance the bullet seat has advanced in the barrel.

<u>f</u>. Reflector, barrel, cal..30 (B147001). - Used for visual inspection of the bore.

<u>g</u>. Scale, steel, graduated. - Used in connection with headspace gage to check headspace.

<u>h</u>. Tool, combination (B.A.R.) (C64145). - Used in disassembling rifle prior to inspection.

<u>i</u>. Tool, cleaning, gas cylinder (C64144). - Used to clean gas cylinder prior to inspection and gaging.

Section IV

INSTRUCTIONS FOR INSPECTION

32. GENERAL. - a. Inspection is for the purpose of determining the condition of the materiel, whether repairs or adjustments are required, and the remedies necessary to insure that the materiel is in serviceable condition. Before inspection is begun, the materiel should be thoroughly cleaned to remove any grease, dirt or other foreign matter which might interfere with its proper functioning. For instructions on cleaning the rifle and materials used, refer to FM 23-15, FM 23-20, section on "Care and Cleaning", TM 9-850, and paragraph 91 of this manual.

b. Inspection, maintenance, and repair of these rifles

should be thorough and exacting, for the malfunction of one small part may cause malfunction of the rifle. A thorough knowledge of disassembly, assembly, functioning and operation of the rifles is most necessary for personnel charged with this work. For instructions in disassembly and assembly, refer to section III of this technical manual. For functioning and operation, refer to FM 23-15 and FM 23-20, sections on "Functioning" and "Operation". For drawings of parts with important contacting surfaces indicated, refer to figures 21, 22, 23 and 24, of this technical manual.

33. INSPECTION REPORT. - The procedure to be followed relating to inspection and maintenance is contained in TM 9-1100, "Ordnance Maintenance Procedure - Materiel Inspection and Repair".

34. INSPECTION OF THE RIFLE AS A UNIT. - a. Inspect rifle as a unit for appearance, rust, corrosion, and general condition.

b. Hand operate and check for functioning and smoothness of operation of assemblies and parts.

c. Test fit of magazine in receiver, and function of magazine catch and catch release with magazine.

d. Using magazine and dummy cartridges, test loading function of bolt and function of extractor and ejector. If neck of ejected cartridge case is dented, it indicates that ejection is weak (casing striking side of receiver), caused by bent neck or worn head of ejector or ejector scraping on bolt. When testing, hold magazine up, as retaining lug may be worn, allowing magazine to drop, thus affecting feed function of bolt.

e. Check locking action of bolt lock and bolt.

f. Fire several rounds of service ammunition and examine primers of fired casings. If primer shows indications of being set back in firing pin hole of bolt, the bolt should be replaced due to enlarged firing pin hole or recessive wear of face of bolt.

CAUTION: Test firing should be done only when and where conditions permit, considering safety and expediency.

g. Check headspace of rifle. Refer to paragraph 48.

h. Check bipod assembly for looseness on flash hider bearing (M1918A2) and gas cylinder tube (M1918A1), and swivel bracket for looseness on gas cylinder tube. Check flash hider for looseness on barrel and spring lock washer (M1918A2). Spring washer should be assembled with spring to front.

i. Check stock rest (M1918A2) for looseness in bearing and butt stock for looseness on receiver and butt plate on butt stock, and hinge and locking action of outer butt plate (M1918A1 and M1918A2).

<u>j</u>. Check butt swivel for looseness on stock rest bushing
(M1918A2) or bracket (M1918 and M1918A1), and bushing or bracket
for looseness on butt stock.

<u>k</u>. Check rear sight base for looseness on receiver, leaf
group on base, front sight base on barrel and leaf in base.

NOTE: Testing parts and assemblies for free movement is
most essential in the inspection of this type of rifle, as
slight binding due to rough, burred or deformed surfaces will
be apparent, which might go unnoticed under spring tension, or
when parts are operating with their assemblies. Free movement
implies that the part or assembly should have an easy, free or
sliding fit, but does not mean that there should be unwarranted
looseness or play which would contribute to malfunction or
hasten wear.

35. BOLT, BOLT LOCK, LINK AND HAMMER GROUP. - <u>a</u>. <u>Function</u>. -
Check free movement of bolt, bolt lock, link and hammer attached
to slide and piston, but with recoil spring disassembled.

(1) <u>Rearward movement</u>. - When bolt is locked, the hammer
pin should be approximately 0.19 in. in advance of the link pin,
and center rib of hammer slightly in rear of head of firing pin.
When slide is retracted it should impart no motion to the bolt
until it has traveled back 0.19 in. from extreme forward position. At this point the hammer pin should be directly under
the bolt link pin. From this point the bolt and bolt lock should
start to move and by the time the slide has traveled 1.20 in.
the bolt lock should be drawn completely down out of the locking
recess and away from locking shoulder of the receiver. As bolt
lock revolves down from locked position, it should cam the firing
pin from the face of the bolt. Slide should continue back until
it strikes buffer and then rebound .10 in. before engaging sear
notch.

(2) <u>Forward movement</u>. - On forward movement, when slide is
about two inches from its forward position, bolt lock should
begin to ride over rear shoulders of bolt supports which cam up
its rear end. The bolt link pin passes over dead center with
respect to bolt lock pin and hammer pin, and the bolt lock is
forced up by link into locking recess in receiver and thus levers
bolt home; the hammer pin passes dead center under bolt link pin.
At this point the firing pin should be released from its slot in
the under side of bolt lock and in position to be struck by
hammer, the hammer moves forward .10 in. and strikes firing pin
head, and then should travel forward another 1/16 in. to its

final forward position. The bolt should be positively locked
by the time the hammer reaches firing pin. For full description
of functioning of above mechanisms, refer to FM 23-15 and FM
23-20, section on "Functioning", and paragraph 48 of this manual
entitled "Headspace".

   b.   Inspection of components. - (1) Bolt (fig. 21). -
Check bolt for excessive side play and looseness with bolt lock,
and bolt lock pin (riveted both ends) and pin for excessive wear
and burs. Check nose for wear and burs, and firing pin hole for
enlargement, face for corrosion and recessive wear. (Refer to
par. 34 f.) Check extractor well for foreign matter and retention under cut for wear and burs. Check firing pin aperture
for rust and foreign matter and firing pin head seating aperture,
and gas escape vents for burs and foreign matter. Check lower
surfaces contacting bolt supports, and center feed rib, for wear
and burs.

   (2) Extractor (fig. 21). - Check extractor for function
and retention in well, and claw for wear and burs. Check extractor spring for fracture, weak action and looseness in extractor body. Claw nose and retaining shoulder should be square,
not beveled.

   (3) Firing pin (fig. 21). - Check firing pin for free
movement in bolt aperture, deformation, rust, worn or burred cam
face, and worn or burred nose and head, and fractured retracting
lug and nose. Firing pin should slide freely in well and pro-
trusion of nose from forward face of bolt should be approximately
3/32 in. If pin enters primer of cartridge too far, it increases
the force necessary to retract the pin, and retracting lug on
head may thus be fractured.

   (4) Bolt lock (fig. 22). - Check bolt lock for excessive
looseness on pin, and with bolt and link. Check rear top shoulder
where lock contacts receiver locking aperture for wear and burs.
This is an important surface. (Refer to headspacing.) Check
lower rear cam surface where lock rides up on bolt supports and
firing pin camming surface for wear and burs.

   (5) Bolt link. - Check link for excessive looseness with
bolt lock and hammer, wear and burs in pin holes, worn pin, and
for burs. When assembled, link should bear on rear camming face
of bolt lock.

   (6) Hammer (fig. 22). - Check hammer for excessive looseness with link, and slide, loose and worn pin, wear and burs.
Check center rib of hammer, which strikes head of firing pin,
for wear and burs. Hammer must be assembled to link with flat

side down.

36. TRIGGER MECHANISM GROUP (figs. 18, 19 and 20). - a. Inspect trigger mechanism group for looseness, function and co-function of its assemblies and parts.

b. M1918A2. - (1) Check function of trigger, connector and sear spring with trigger mechanism held horizontal, tipped forward and tipped back. If sear spring is not bearing properly on forward shoulders of sear and center prong on connector, the connector will not function properly when mechanism is tipped. Check function of trigger, sear and stop lever, when change lever is set at A (normal cyclic rate), F (slow cyclic rate), and S (safe).

(2) When change lever is set at A (vertical position), and trigger is retracted, the connector should raise the forward end of sear and sear release stop lever together and hold them up as long as trigger is held fully retracted. Thus the rear end of the sear is depressed and held from engagement with sear notch in slide, while rear end of sear end of sear release stop lever is only partially depressed, thus still preventing sear release from striking camming surface on rear end of sear. When trigger is released, sear and sear release stop lever should both return to their normal positions.

(3) When change lever is set at F (forward position) and trigger partially retracted, the connector should raise the forward end of sear and sear release stop lever together. As trigger is further retracted, the connector, still rising, should be cammed from under rear end of sear by camming surface on sear carrier, and continue to raise forward end of sear release stop lever, and hold it in raised position as long as trigger is held fully retracted. Thus sear is free to function vertically and be acted upon by the sear release, while the sear release stop lever is depressed to a point where it will not block the action of the sear release upon the camming surface of rear end of sear, and thus produces the slow cyclic rate of fire.

(4) When change lever is set at S (rear position) the trigger should be blocked and thus prevented from lifting the connector and thus disengaging the sear. For further explanation, refer to FM 23-15, section on "Functioning".

c. M1918 and M1918A1. - (1) Check function of trigger and sear when change lever is set at A (automatic), F (semi-automatic) and S (safe).

(2) When change lever is set at A, (vertical position),

and trigger retracted, the connector should raise the forward end of sear, thus depressing the rear end and holding the sear out of engagement, as long as trigger is held fully retracted.

(3) When change lever is set at F, (forward position) and trigger partially retracted, the connector should raise the front end of the sear, thus depressing rear end. As trigger is retracted farther, the connector is cammed from under sear by cam on the sear carrier, thus giving sear free vertical movement, and the rear end should rise again. When trigger is released, the connector should return to lowered position through action of sear spring (center leaf) to be in position to raise front end of sear when trigger is again retracted.

(4) When change lever is set at S (rear position), trigger should be blocked and thus prevented from raising the connector and disengaging the sear.

d. <u>Trigger group</u> (fig. 23). - Check trigger for looseness and free movement on trigger pin; pin for looseness in trigger guard body, wear, and burs. Check trigger for full pivoting action on pin with respect to guard. Check connector pin for looseness in trigger (riveted) and connector aperture and pin for wear and burs. Check heel of trigger for wear and burs. Top rear corner should be sharp, not beveled, at point where it enters notch in change lever. Check heel and tip of trigger for sufficient clearance with bow of guard for full retraction.

e. <u>Connector</u> (fig. 23). - Check connector for looseness in trigger, wear and burs in pin seating notch. Check top bearing surface where it contacts sear, and stop lever (M1918A2). This is a critical surface, as excessive wear or burs may affect function of sear and stop. Check rear toe of connector where it contacts tongue in change lever aperture for wear and burs. Check top front sloping surface (sear spring ramp) and rear sloping surface below top flat (sear carrier ramp) for wear and burs.

f. <u>Sear and sear spring</u> (figs. 21 and 23). - (1) Check sear for looseness on pin, pin for undue wear at ends and for burs. (Wear of pin at ends is increased due to movement in elongated hole in trigger guard.) Check sear for free movement (should be easy fit) in sear carrier, deformation, wear and burs on forward lower camming surface contacting connector, and on rear upper camming surface (M1918A2) contacting sear release. Check sear notch faces (rear and top) for wear and burs. Edge should be sharp and clean. (Refer to par. 88 for stoning.)

NOTE: Sear pin holes in trigger guard and trigger pin

SEMIAUTOMATIC POSITION (F)

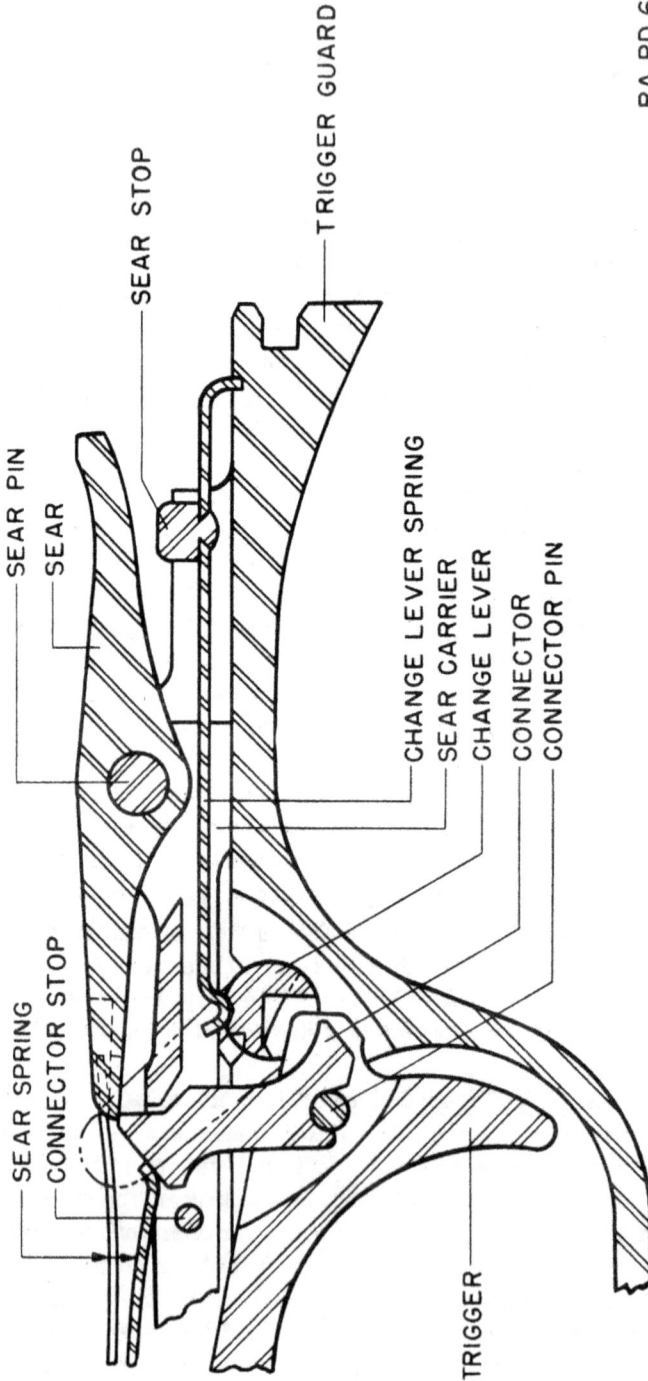

SEAR PIN
SEAR
SEAR STOP
SEAR SPRING
CONNECTOR STOP
CHANGE LEVER SPRING
SEAR CARRIER
CHANGE LEVER
CONNECTOR
CONNECTOR PIN
TRIGGER GUARD
TRIGGER

RA PD 6095

FIGURE 18—BROWNING AUTOMATIC RIFLE, CAL. .30, M1918 AND M1918A1 - TRIGGER AND SEAR GROUP - SECTIONAL VIEW - LEFT SIDE - CHANGE LEVER SET AT "F", SEMI-AUTOMATIC FIRE M1918 AND M1918A1, SLOW CYCLIC RATE M1918A2

AUTOMATIC POSITION (A)

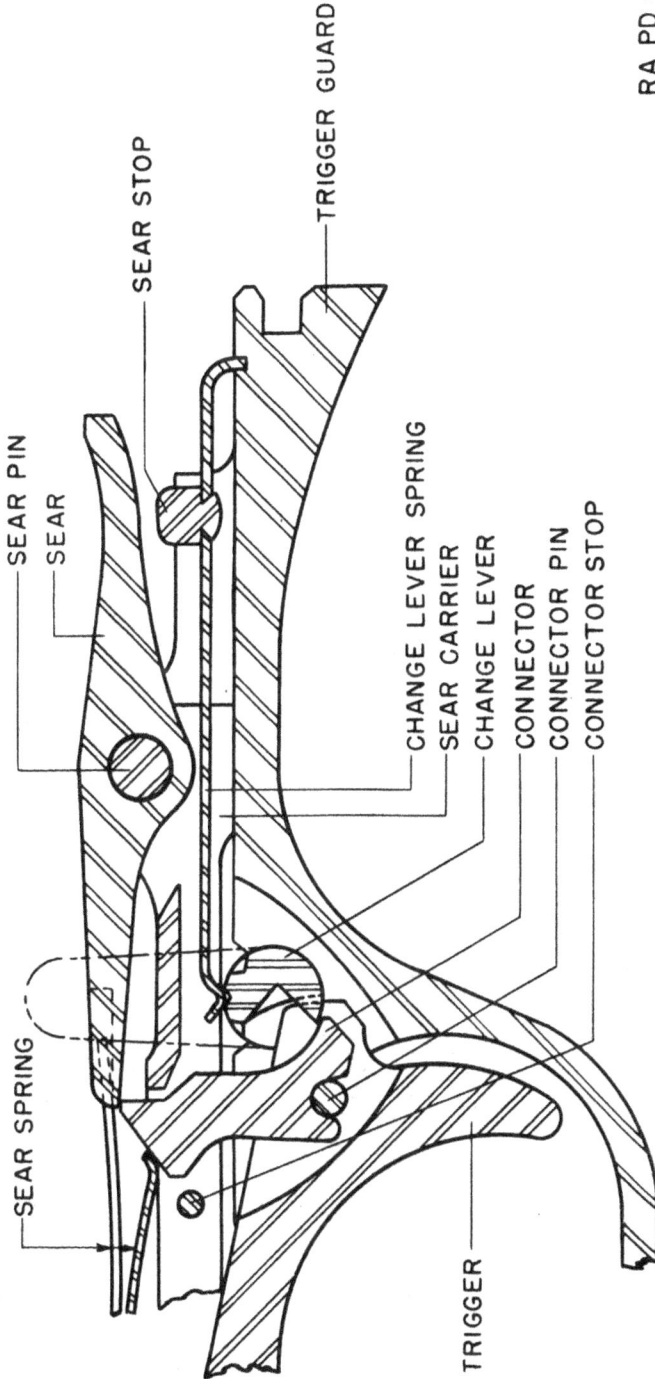

SEAR PIN

SEAR

SEAR SPRING

SEAR STOP

TRIGGER GUARD

CHANGE LEVER SPRING

SEAR CARRIER

CHANGE LEVER

CONNECTOR

CONNECTOR PIN

CONNECTOR STOP

TRIGGER

RA PD 6096

FIGURE 19 — BROWNING AUTOMATIC RIFLE, CAL. .30, M1918 AND M1918A1 - TRIGGER AND SEAR GROUP - SECTIONAL VIEW - LEFT SIDE - CHANGE LEVER SET AT "A", AUTOMATIC FIRE M1918 AND M1918A1, NORMAL CYCLIC RATE M1918A2

43

SAFE POSITION (S)

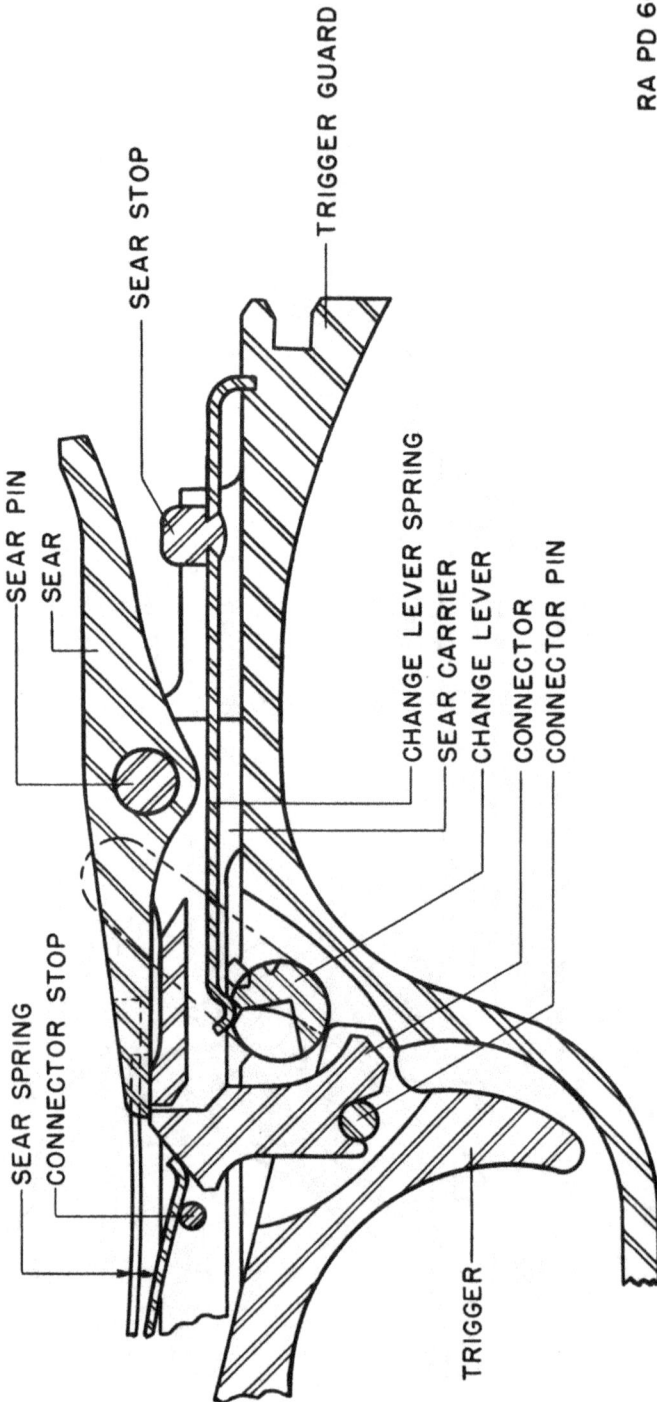

SEAR PIN
SEAR
SEAR STOP
TRIGGER GUARD
CHANGE LEVER SPRING
SEAR CARRIER
CHANGE LEVER
CONNECTOR
CONNECTOR PIN
SEAR SPRING
CONNECTOR STOP
TRIGGER

RA PD 6097

FIGURE 20 — BROWNING AUTOMATIC RIFLE, CAL. .30, M1918 AND M1918A1 - TRIGGER AND SEAR GROUP -
SECTIONAL VIEW - LEFT SIDE - CHANGE LEVER SET AT "S", SAFE POSITION, ALL TYPES

holes in sear carrier are elongated to allow play of mechanism, relative to counterrecoil spring, to absorb jar of counterrecoil on the mechanism.

(2) Check sear spring for function with sear and connector, looseness in retaining slots in trigger guard body, deformation and fracture. The two side prongs of spring should bear evenly on shoulders on forward end of sear. Center prong should lie below forward end of stop lever and bear on forward ramp of connector. Prongs are even when at rest, and curved downward. Forward end of spring should be well seated in its lateral notch in trigger guard body.

g. Sear release stop lever (M1918A2) (fig. 23). - Check stop lever for deformation, free movement with sear, looseness on sear pin and in sear (should be easy fit). Check for wear and burs on forward lower surface where it contacts connector, and on rear surface where sear release strikes. Rear nose may become expanded due to action of sear release, and thus bind in sear.

h. Sear carrier and counterrecoil spring (fig. 23). - Check sear carrier for deformation, burs in trigger pin holes (elongated), and loose, fractured, worn, or burred connector stop (riveted on right end). Check counterrecoil spring guide for deformation, free movement in trigger guard aperture, wear, and burs on nose. Check sear pin hole for wear and burs. Check connector camming surface for wear and burs. Check counterrecoil spring for function, fracture and set. Free length of spring (B147136) is .77 -.02 in.

i. Change lever (fig. 24). - Check change lever for function with connector and trigger, deformation and free movement in trigger guard body (should be close fit). Check locking lug, connector tongue, and aperture for wear and burs. Check lateral (change lever spring) retention notches for retentive function, wear and burs, and lever arm friction notches for wear. Check change lever stop for function with change lever.

j. Change and stop lever spring (M1918A2). - Check change and stop lever spring for function with change lever (should bear firmly in notches), and sear release stop lever, looseness in trigger guard body retaining aperture, deformation and cracks. Check stop lever prong for fracture, looseness on rivet and excessive deformation, causing weak action on stop lever.

k. Change lever spring (M1918 and M1918A1). - Check change lever spring for function with change lever (should bear firmly in notches) and looseness in trigger guard body retaining aperture. Check sear stop for looseness (riveted) on spring, function with sear, wear and burs. Check spring for deformation and cracks.

1. Magazine catch group (fig. 24). - Check magazine catch for looseness on pin and pin for looseness in trigger guard body, and for wear and burs. Check nose of catch for wear and burs (edge should be sharp). Check spring recess and release aperture for wear, burs, and foreign matter. Check catch release for free movement in trigger guard body and catch, deformation, fractured nose, wear and burs and aperture for foreign matter. Check spring for function, fracture and set. Free length of spring (B147134) is .44 -.04 in.

m. Ejector group (fig. 24). - Check ejector for deformation, undue looseness in trigger guard body and with lock, and worn lock aperture. Check nose of ejector for deformation, wear and burs. Upper forward corner of nose should be well defined. If nose is bent or worn, it will fail to eject properly; if too long, it will bind on bolt and cause weak ejection. Check ejector lock for free movement in well in trigger guard housing, well for foreign matter, and lock nose for wear and burs. Check spring for function, fracture and set. Free length of spring (B147135) is .77 -.04 in.

n. Trigger guard body and magazine guides. - Check trigger guard body for deformation, wear in pin holes (sear pin hole is elongated), worn and burred spring retaining grooves and receiver retention groove (rear end). Check magazine guides for deformation and looseness, screws for looseness (staked), and for burs.

37. GAS CYLINDER TUBE BRACKET. - Check gas cylinder tube bracket for looseness on barrel, missing or loose pin, coincidence of gas port with barrel port, and for worn and burred dovetail mating grooves. (Bracket is drive fit on barrel, and gas port is drilled through bracket and barrel after assembly at manufacture.)

38. GAS CYLINDER TUBE, FOREARM AND FRONT SWIVEL GROUP. - a. Tube. - Check gas cylinder tube for looseness in tube bracket, and worn and burred dovetail. Dovetail tapers to rear and must be assembled to bracket from front end. Check gas port for coincidence with bracket port, carbon and foreign matter, and surface of dovetail contacting bracket for rust and corrosion. Check rear tang for mating with aperture in receiver, wear, and burs. (If barrel is not alined properly with receiver, or if tube is deformed, this tang will not slide into aperture freely.) Check retaining pin hole for wear and burs, tube for dents, burs

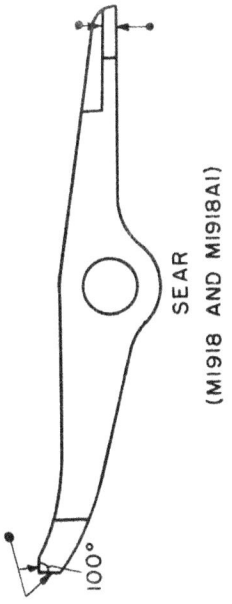

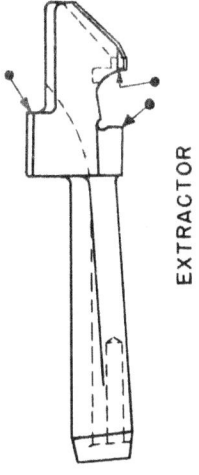

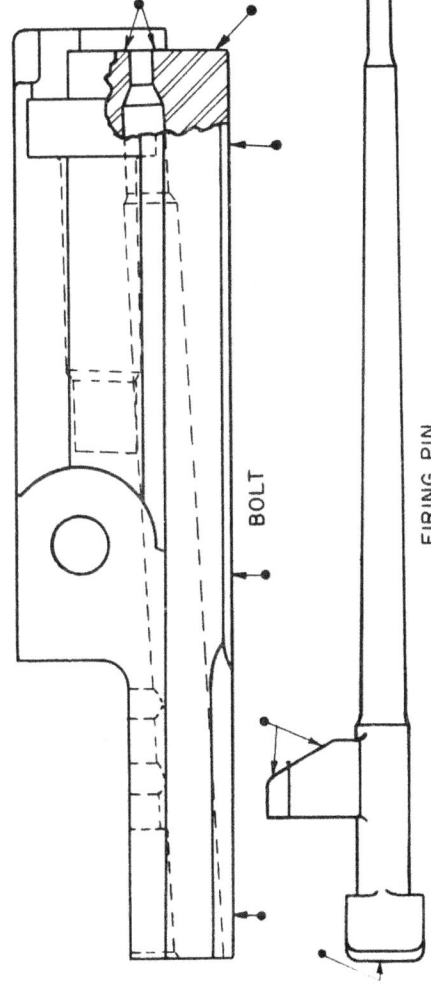

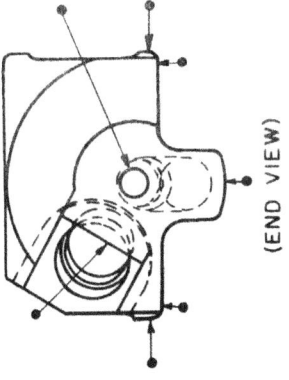

EXTRACTOR

(END VIEW)

RA PD 6098

SEAR
(M1918 AND M1918A1)

100°

BOLT

FIRING PIN

FIGURE 21 — BROWNING AUTOMATIC RIFLE, CAL. .30 - PARTS -
IMPORTANT CONTACTING SURFACES INDICATED BY ARROWS

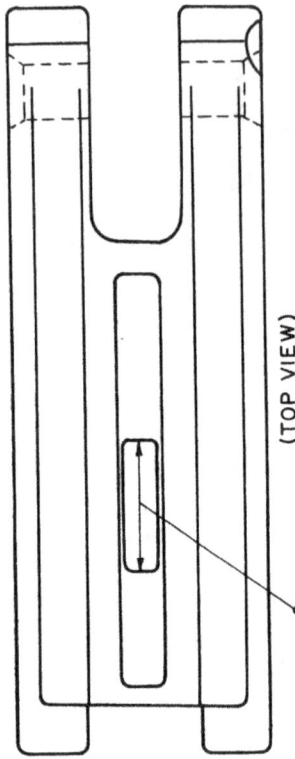
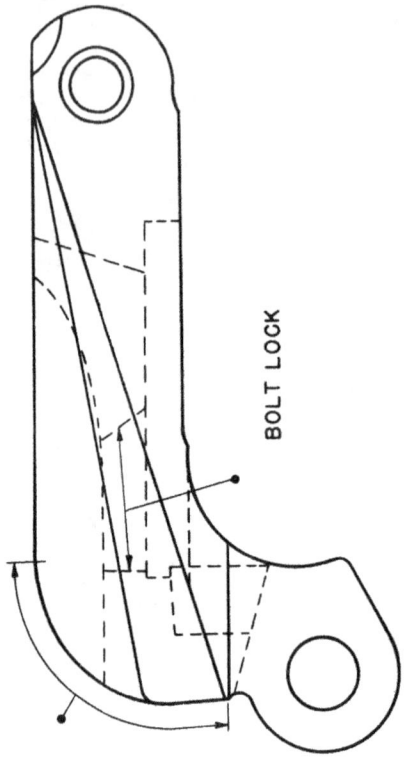

(TOP VIEW)

BOLT LOCK

RA PD 6099

FIGURE 22 — BROWNING AUTOMATIC RIFLE, CAL. .30 - PARTS -
IMPORTANT CONTACTING SURFACES INDICATED BY ARROWS

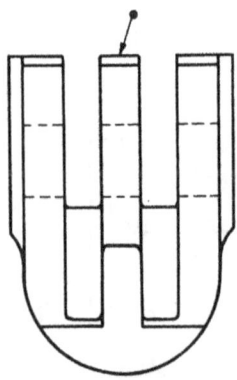

(TOP VIEW)

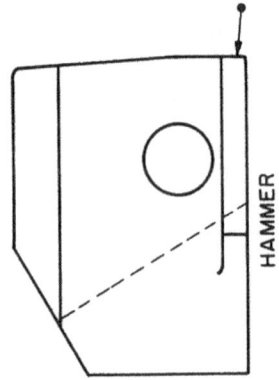

HAMMER

48

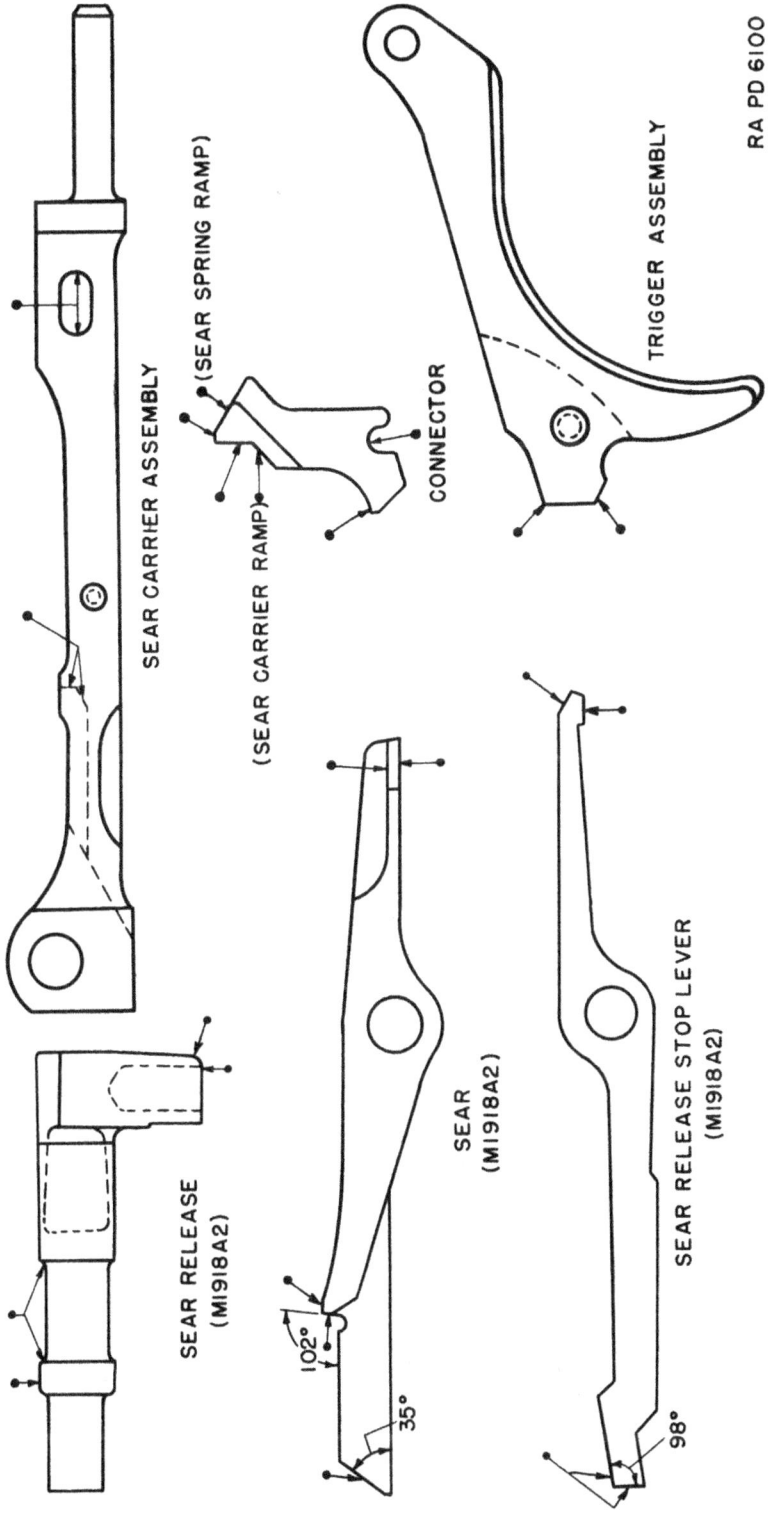

FIGURE 23 — BROWNING AUTOMATIC RIFLE, CAL. .30 - PARTS - IMPORTANT CONTACTING SURFACES INDICATED BY ARROWS

SEAR CARRIER ASSEMBLY

(SEAR SPRING RAMP)

(SEAR CARRIER RAMP)

CONNECTOR

TRIGGER ASSEMBLY

RA PD 6100

SEAR RELEASE
(M1918A2)

SEAR
(M1918A2)

SEAR RELEASE STOP LEVER
(M1918A2)

102°

35°

98°

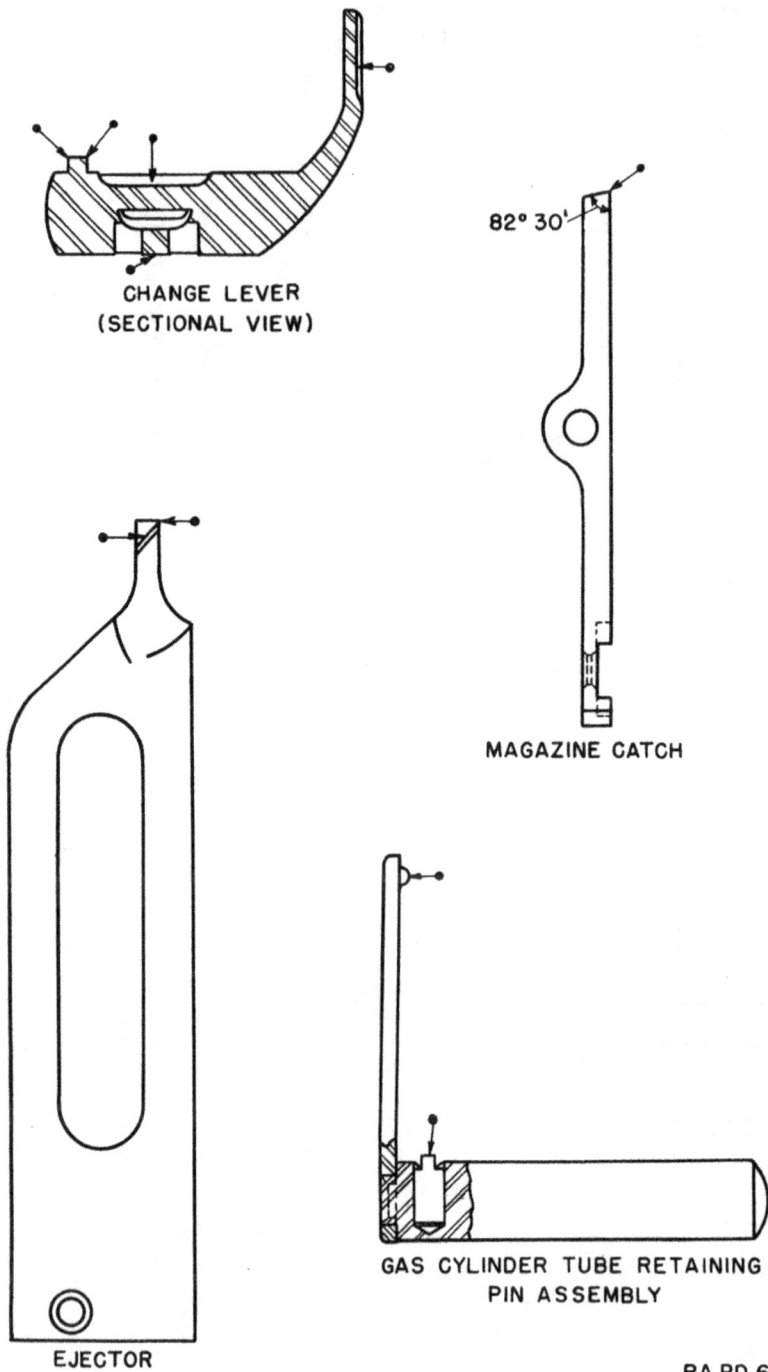

CHANGE LEVER
(SECTIONAL VIEW)

82° 30'

MAGAZINE CATCH

EJECTOR

GAS CYLINDER TUBE RETAINING
PIN ASSEMBLY

RA PD 6101

FIGURE 24 — BROWNING AUTOMATIC RIFLE, CAL. .30 - PARTS -
IMPORTANT CONTACTING SURFACES INDICATED BY ARROWS

and rust on interior and exterior. Tube should be smooth and polished inside. Check the six gas escape ports for foreign matter, and tube barrel riding lugs (top) for burs.

b. _Gas cylinder tube retaining pin assembly_ (fig. 24). - Check pin for spring retention with depression in receiver, locking function of key in undercut in receiver (left side). Check key for looseness in pin (staked), fracture, wear, and burs. Check spring for looseness on pin (riveted), deformation, or fracture. If spring becomes loose from pin, pin cannot be rotated to be withdrawn from receiver. (Refer to par. 83.)

c. _Gas cylinder group_. - (1) **General inspection**. - Check gas cylinder for looseness in tube, and for missing, fractured, or loose lock. Check lock for spring action and burs. (To remove lock, use needle nose pliers. To replace, insert in groove and rotate down until caught.) Check variable gas ports for carbon and foreign matter and cylinder and tube for crossed threads, wear and burs. Check gas pressure relief vent in head of cylinder for carbon and foreign matter.

(2) _Gaging_. - Check gas cylinder for wear using gas cylinder gage A77204. This is a "no-go" gage and should not enter the gas cylinder. It is to be used on both old and new type gas cylinders. Before testing the cylinder, clean thoroughly to remove all carbon deposits and foreign matter, using gas cylinder cleaning tool. Use crocus cloth to polish if necessary. Wipe cylinder and gage with slightly oiled rag and try to insert the gage into the cylinder. If the gage enters cylinder, it is unserviceable and should be replaced. Gas cylinder gage (A77202), previously issued for use with gas cylinders of early manufacture, is no longer authorized and should not be used.

NOTE: New type of gas cylinders, having a relief vent in head, are larger in bore diameter than old type without relief vent, to give more piston clearance.

d. _Forearm group_. - Check wood forearm for looseness on gas cylinder tube, loose screws and escutcheon, scoring, cracks, and worn checkering. Check shield grooves (M1918A2) for wear and cracks, and shield for deformation, dents and burs on slides. Shield should be assembled with aperture to rear, and convex side towards gas cylinder tube.

e. _Front swivel group_. - Check front swivel bracket for looseness on gas cylinder tube. Should be positioned firmly just ahead of forearm. Check screw for looseness, wear, and burs, and swivel for looseness, deformation, wear, and burs.

39. SLIDE, PISTON AND RECOIL SPRING GROUP. - a. _General_

<u>inspection</u>. - Check free action of piston and slide with respect to gas cylinder, tube, and receiver. Piston and slide should slide freely in gas cylinder, tube and receiver when gun is tilted with recoil spring disassembled. Check piston retaining pin for looseness and wear in piston and slide. Articular movement between piston and slide is allowed, when assembled, to insure proper alinement and free movement of slide assembly in receiver. For replacement, piston and slide are furnished undrilled. Piston is assembled to slide and then backed off sufficiently to allow slight play and free alinement, then drilled for pin and pin assembled.

<u>b</u>. <u>Slide</u>. - Check slide for excess looseness with piston, deformation of sides by pinching or springing, which causes binding with operating mechanism or receiver, badly dented rear end (indicating frozen buffer), worn hammer pin hole, wear, and burs.

<u>c</u>. <u>Piston</u>. - (1) Check piston for deformation, wear and burs on head, and gas check bearing rings. Check plug for looseness in head. When assembled, plug lies below face of piston. This recess should be checked for rust and carbon. Check piston tube for missing or fractured bushing. (This bushing is sprung into cut inside of tube and acts as a bearing stop for the recoil spring. It is assembled at manufacture and should not be removed. If damaged, replace piston assembly.) Check piston for carbon and rust. Bearing surfaces should be smooth and polished; use crocus cloth if necessary.

(2) Gage piston head with piston gage (A77201) for wear. This gage is a "no-go" gage and piston head should not enter gage. To gage, first clean piston thoroughly of all carbon and fouling and see that surfaces of head rings are smooth and polished. Wipe piston head and gage with slightly oily rag and try to pass gage over piston head (plug end). If piston enters gage, it is unserviceable and should be scrapped.

<u>d</u>. <u>Recoil spring and guide</u>. - Check recoil spring for function, fracture, kinks, and set, and spring guide for deformation, wear and burs on flanges of head, loose head (riveted), fit, and retention in retaining shoulders in receiver, and for worn checkering of head. (This part is used as a tool in disassembly and is apt to become deformed or damaged.) Free length of recoil spring (B147131) is 16.0 -1.0 in. If spring is set more than one inch, or is kinked, it should be replaced.

40. BUFFER AND SEAR RELEASE GROUP (M1918A2). - <u>a</u>. Test reciprocation of buffer head with buffer spring and for free

movement in buffer tube. Check tube for position and looseness
in receiver, and worn or burred head keyways. Check buffer
qualifying shim for fracture and wear. This shim is split and
.005 in. in thickness. Buffer tube and receiver are qualified
at assembly so keyways aline properly with receiver. One of
the eight keyways in forward end of buffer tube should be centered
and parallel with top of receiver, so as to position sear release
vertically with nose down when buffer head is assembled. Key
in buffer head positions head and limits horizontal forward
movement of sear release.

   _b_. Check cap for looseness in tube and tube for deformation,
dents, crossed threads, wear, burs, and foreign matter. Check
buffer head, four cups and four cones for free action in tube.
Check cones for expansion seating in mating cups (cones should not
seat fully in cups when at rest), and for cracks, wear, burs,
and foreign matter.

   _c_. Check buffer key for looseness in buffer tube and
head, wear, and burs (both ends). Check sear release aperture
in buffer head for wear and burs at forward edges. Check pro-
trusion of buffer head from face of tube. This dimension should
be approximately 1/8 in. Check buffer spring for function,
fracture and set. Free length of spring (B147133) is 1.27 -.04
in. When removing buffer tube, spot tube and receiver withdraw
mark for convenience in assembling.

   _d_. Sear release (fig. 23). - Check sear release for free
movement in buffer head (should be flush with buffer head forward
face when retracted) excess looseness or binding in notch, worn
and burred bearing surfaces and buffer key retaining shoulders.
Check camming face of nose for wear and burs. Lower forward
edge of nose should be slightly beveled.

   41. BUFFER GROUP (M1918 and M1918A1). - Test reciprocation
of buffer with buffer spring and for free movement in tube.
Check tube for looseness in receiver, deformation, dents, wear
and burs and nut for looseness in tube and crossed threads.
Check four buffer cups and four cones for free action in tube
and cones for free seating in mating cups (cones should not
seat fully in cup when at rest), and for cracks, wear, burs,
and foreign matter. Check butt stock bolt for looseness in
buffer nut and for wear and burs, and washer for wear and burs.
Check buffer spring for function, fracture and set. Free length
of spring (B147133) is 1.27 -.04 in.

   42. ACTUATOR GROUP (M1918A2). - Test actuator and sear
release for co-function under spring action, and sear release

with sear and sear release stop lever. Check free movement
of sear release in buffer head (should be easy fit), and for
excessive looseness, wear and burs. Check actuator tube for
looseness in buffer cap, deformation, dents, wear, burs on forward
edge, and foreign matter. (Tube is locked to cap by brass wire
ring fitting in groove in cap, brazed to tube and cap after
assembly.) Tube should be smooth and polished inside. Use
wire cleaning brush, cal..30, if necessary. Check free movement of actuator in actuator tube (should slide freely) and
for wear and burs. Actuator should be assembled with blunt
end forward. Check actuator spring for function, fracture and
set. Free length of spring (B147496) is 11 ±1/8 in.

43. STOCK RETAINING SLEEVE GROUP (M1918A2). - Check stock
retaining sleeve for looseness with actuator tube, and looseness
of stop in sleeve and collar on sleeve. Stop is pinned and
brazed in rear end of sleeve, and collar is brazed to forward
end of sleeve by same method employed in brazing actuator tube
in buffer cap. (Refer to par. 42.) Stock retaining sleeve
screws on end of actuator tube by means of mating threads on stop
and in tube. Hole in stop is air compression relief vent. Check
stock retaining sleeve lock washer for locking function, cracks,
and wear. Washer should be assembled with locking prong to the
rear. Check stop tool slot for wear and burs.

44. RECEIVER. - Check receiver for deformation (pinched
sides due to squeezing in vise), rust, loose, worn and burred
left and right bolt supports, loose rivets, and cracks in barrel
end and bridge. Check buffer tube and barrel threads crossing,
wear, and burs. Check change lever stop spring apertures and
pin hole, and bolt guide spring aperture for wear and burs.
Check operating handle slideways for wear and burs. Check bolt
lock recess in top for wavy surface, wear, and burs, especially
where lock seats when bolt is locked. Surface can be inspected
by reflecting light on it from small mirror or bright tool. This
surface is critical and affects headspace. Check top plate for
looseness and burs (should be a drive fit) and plate grooves in
receiver and mating flanges of top plate for wear and burs.
Check gas tube mating tang aperture for wear and burs. Check
rear sight base dovetail grooves and set screw aperture for
wears and burs.

45. BOLT GUIDE AND CHANGE LEVER STOP. - a. Bolt guide. -
Check bolt guide for sustaining function with bolt, looseness
with spring, looseness of spring in receiver aperture, weak
spring action, wear, and burs.

<u>b</u>. <u>Change lever stop</u>. - Check change lever stop for function with spring, stop for wear and burs, looseness on spring (riveted) and weak spring. Check spring for looseness in receiver aperture, and pin for looseness, wear, and burs.

46. OPERATING HANDLE. - Check operating handle for function and free movement in its slideway, wear and burs on sliding surfaces, and in hammer pin aperture. Check spring plunger well for foreign matter, plunger for function and free movement in well, wear and burs. Check plunger spring for function, fracture and set. Free length of spring (B147132) is .600 -.100 in.

NOTE: Operating handle must be assembled with knob forward. Projection on rear end is to prevent incorrect assembly and should not be removed. If handle is assembled incorrectly, hammer pin and handle cannot be removed except by drilling handle. Refer to paragraph 84.

47. BARREL. - <u>a</u>. Inspect barrel generally and for serviceability.

<u>b</u>. <u>General inspection</u>. - Check barrel for deformation, alinement in receiver, crossed threads, rust, corrosion, wear and burs, and foreign matter in gas port and extractor aperture. Barrel must aline exactly with receiver when assembled in order that rear end of gas cylinder tube will fit mating slot in receiver, front sight will aline properly, and extractor aperture will be correctly positioned. Gas cylinder tube bracket and front sight base are positioned, drilled and pinned during manufacture of the rifle, after barrel is assembled to receiver. A draw mark is then placed on barrel and receiver for proper alinement upon reassembly. If draw marks will not qualify, a shim can be fashioned from shim metal, or barrel may be lightly peened. (Refer to par. 77.)

<u>c</u>. <u>Inspection for serviceability</u>. - (1) Inspection of barrels for serviceability will, in general, be based on accuracy, and inspectors will be guided by this requirement. For ordinary inspection barrel will not be removed from receiver. Barrel will only be removed for changing, or to determine excessive depth of chamber. Accuracy is reduced in varying degrees by the following defects; bulges, erosion, and pits. The extent to which these defects reduce accuracy is determined by visual inspection and bore gaging. Before any attempt is made to inspect barrel for serviceability, metal and all other fouling should be removed and bore wiped dry.

(2) <u>Visual inspection</u>. - (<u>a</u>) Hold barrel so its interior

will be lighted. If barrel is not disassembled from receiver, use inspector's bore reflector. Examine bore from muzzle to breech. If bore appears free from bulges and pits, and lands are sharp and uniformly distinct, the barrel is serviceable with regard to bore.

(b) If the barrel contains small pits, but has sharp, uniformly distinct lands and is free from bulges and excessive wear in chamber, it will be sufficiently accurate to be serviceable.

(c) If barrel contains a bulge, it is unserviceable and should be scrapped. This condition is indicated by a shadowy depression or dark ring in bore and/or bulge or raised ring on barrel surface.

(d) If barrel is pitted to extent that sharpness of lands is affected, or if it has a pit or pits in lands or grooves, large enough to permit passage of gas past the bullet, i.e., a pit the width of a land or groove and 3/8 to 1/2 in. long, it is, or soon will be, too inaccurate for serviceability and should be scrapped. This condition implies that proper care of the barrel in accordance with methods prescribed in FM 23-15, FM 23-20, and TM 9-850, has not been taken, and period of serviceability will be lessened.

(e) Each barrel inspected and found serviceable by visual inspection and barrels considered unserviceable by visual inspection due to wear at the origin of the rifling will be bore gaged using breech bore gage C3940. This gage is also used with cal..30 machine guns, and the M1903 and M1903A1 rifles, and is now manufactured in two pieces. Disassemble the rifle and with the handle removed from the gage, insert it into the barrel through the bottom of the receiver. The rifle should be turned on its side with the ejection opening up. The breech bore reading should be taken through this opening. Compare the graduations with the exposed portion of the barrel; if the gage reads .310 in. or more the barrel is unserviceable. The first graduations on the gage which are for use with machine guns should be used. Pits in a barrel classed as unserviceable under this condition will be disregarded.

(f) Attention should be paid to the chamber of the barrel to see that the depth is not excessive. In cases where the depth of the chamber is excessive the barrel should be scrapped. If shells of fired cartridges are split at necking, it indicates excessive length or enlargement.

(g) To determine whether or not the depth of the chamber

is excessive, remove the barrel as explained in paragraph 18, and place the 1.940 in. headspace gage in the chamber, and with a depth gage find the dimension from the face of the head-space gage to the base of the barrel. If this dimension is less than 0.075 in., the barrel should be scrapped.

(h) In reassembling barrel to receiver, particular attention should be paid to alinement (draw) marks. After qualifying alinement marks, a gas cylinder tube should be tried to insure alinement of gas cylinder tube bracket with receiver. Gas cylinder tubes are not generally interchangeable.

48. HEADSPACE. - a. As a means of verifying the headspace in the Browning automatic rifle, the following gage test is prescribed: Rifles that have been cleaned and repaired by ordnance maintenance personnel or in shops, will be tested with the 1.940-in. and 1.946-in. headspace gages. For the test of rifles in service, the 1.940-in. and the 1.950-in. gages will be used.

b. Excessive headspace is caused in the Browning automatic rifle by wearing away of the locking shoulder of the bolt lock, recessive wear of the face of bolt, a deep or worn chamber, and wear in locking recess of receiver. It can be corrected by replacing the bolt assembly, bolt or bolt lock, barrel, or receiver. Replacement of the bolt lock will be by selection from a number of bolt locks and/or bolts owing to the variation of the bolts and other components of the rifle. Before attempting selective assembly of bolt lock or bolt, selective assembly of bolt assembly should be tried. If neither of these tests corrects headspace, it may be assumed that the fault lies in excessive depth of barrel chamber or in receiver locking recess, and the chamber should next be checked. (Refer to par. 78.)

c. To check headspace, disassemble the rifle and remove the firing pin and extractor from the bolt. With the inspector's bore reflector examine the chamber and make sure it is clean. Place the bolt assembly and bolt link (assembled) in the receiver. Then replace the slide and fit the hammer into its seat. Now aline the holes in the hammer, bolt link and slide, and insert the hammer pin. Work the slide back and forth several times to insure that the parts are correctly assembled. With slide fully forward, note the relative position of the hammer pin with reference to the forward part of its slot in the side of the receiver. It will be found that there is a clearance of from 1/32 to 3/64 in. between the hammer pin and the forward part of the slot. This position of the hammer pin is referred to hereafter as the "locked position".

d. Test of cleaned and repair rifles. - (1) Retract slide and place the 1.940-in. headspace gage in the chamber and move the slide fully forward. Note the position of the hammer pin. It should be in the "locked position". If the hammer pin is in the "locked position" the minimum headspace is correct. Any slight binding of the mechanism during the above operation should be disregarded. Move the slide to the rear and remove the gage.

(2) Place the 1.946-in. headspace gage in the chamber and move the slide forward. Note the position of the hammer pin. It should be not less than 3/8 in. from the "locked position". If the hammer pin is not stopped at or before it is in this position, the headspace is excessive and should be corrected as described in paragraphs 48 b and 78.

e. Test of rifles in service. - (1) The test for minimum headspace of rifles in service is made as already explained for cleaned and repaired rifles.

(2) To test for maximum headspace, place the 1.950-in. headspace gage in the chamber and move the slide forward. Note position of the hammer pin. It should be not less than 3/8 in. from the "locked position". If the hammer pin is not stopped at or before it is in this position, the headspace is excessive and should be corrected as described in paragraphs 48 b and 78.

49. BUTT STOCK AND SWIVEL GROUP. - a. Check butt stock for looseness on receiver, cracks, scoring, surfaces protruding beyond metal, binding of operating handle groove, and dry wood. (Refer to par. 66.) Check screw holes for worn or stripped threads, and apertures for foreign matter.

b. Check stock rest bushing and swivel bracket (M1918A2), or swivel bracket (M1918 and M1918A1) for looseness on butt stock, and bushing or bracket screws for looseness, wear, and burs. Check swivel for deformation, excessive looseness on bushing or bracket, and loose, worn and burred swivel screw and mating threads. Swivel screws are staked at assembly. Check stock rest aperture in bushing (M1918A2) for worn locking shoulder burs.

50. BUTT PLATE GROUP. - a. Check butt plate for looseness on butt stock, level seating, loose hinge lug (M1918A1 and M1918A2), deformation, dents and burs. Check screws for looseness, wear and burs. Check mating screw threads in butt stock for stripping. (Refer to par. 68.)

b. Check lock set screw for looseness, wear and burs,

ball for uneven seating in aperture and burs, and spring for function, fracture, and set. Free length of spring (A13747) is 11/16 -1/32 in.

c. Check trap for function, seating in butt plate (should be flush), looseness, deformation, loose axis pin (staked both ends), weakness of trap spring, and loose, worn, or burred spring screw.

d. Check outer butt plate (long, M1918A1, rifles of early manufacture, and short, M1918A1, rifles of recent manufacture, and M1918A2 rifles), for deformation, seating on inner butt plate (should lie close), cracks, looseness on hinge pin, and loose and worn hinge pin (staked both ends).

e. Check the two locking ball apertures for wear and burs. Check locking action of outer plate (M1918A1 and M1918A2) in vertical and horizontal position and retaining function of lock.

51. FRONT SIGHT GROUP. - Check front sight base for looseness on barrel, missing, loose or burred key, and worn keyway (in barrel). Check for missing front sight key pin, looseness of pin in base and with key. Check front sight blade for position (staked), looseness in base mating dovetail, worn or burred dovetail (male and female), deformation and shine. When assembling new blade it should be alined by eye and staked into position.

52. BIPOD GROUP (M1918A2). - a. Function. - Check bipod for looseness on flash hider (bearing); should be "push on" fit. (Friction washer gives holding tension on bearing and spring on bipod but if bipod is too snug a fit, expansion of flash hider due to heating may cause locking.) Check spring washer for function with bipod, loose or broken washer spring on washer body (tack welded), and washer for wear and burs. Washer should be assembled to barrel with spring forward. Check clamping thumb screws for locking function, worn threads, and burs. Check folding and locking action of legs, and sliding and locking of sliding legs.

b. Body. - Check bipod body for deformation of cylinder, and leg locking slots, wear, cracks, and burs.

c. Leg (left and right). - Check leg joint for looseness on tube, (welded), loose fit in body mating apertures, locking action, wear, and burs. Check tubes for deformation, dents, and burs. Check leg clamp for looseness on tube (welded), spring action, and worn or burred threads. Check clamp thumb screws for function, deformation, looseness in clamp, worn threads, and for burs. Check (floating) key for fracture, deformation, wear, and burs.

d. Sliding leg (left and right). - Check sliding leg for binding or excessive looseness in leg tube; should slide freely without binding or shake. Check tube for deformation, keyway for wear and foreign matter, loose and deformed foot (welded), and for wear and burs.

53. BIPOD GROUP (M1918A1). - a. Function. - Check bipod for looseness on gas cylinder. Test hinge action of legs and function of catch, sliding legs, clamps, stop, and thumb screws. Legs should fold forward along barrel and be retained in position firmly by catch positioned on left leg.

b. Body. - Check body for wear causing looseness on gas cylinder, damaged threads, and for burs; should be firm and secure when screws are drawn down. Check body screws for up-setting (if assembled), looseness, wear, and burs. Check leg hinge slots for deformation (pinched or spread), wear and burs, and rod end pin holes for wear.

c. Hinged leg (left and right). - Check leg hinge for looseness in bipod body and on rod end pin, and pin for looseness, damaged or missing cotter pin, and for wear and burs. Check hinge for looseness on tube (welded), tube for deformation, dents and burs, clamp for looseness on tube (welded), worn and burred thumbscrew threads, and worn sliding leg stop pin stop shoulder.

d. Sliding leg (left and right). - Check sliding leg for binding or excessive looseness in hinged leg tube, deformation, dents, loose or missing stop pin, worn stop pin hole, and for burs. Check stop pin for wear and burs. Check foot for loose-ness in sliding leg tube (welded), wear, and burs. Check thumb-screws for wear and burs. Check leg catch (left leg only) for looseness on hinge leg tube (should be firm spring fit), loose rivet, deformation, and burs.

54. STOCK REST GROUP (M1918A2). - a. Function. - Check stock rest for looseness and loose retention in bushing, function of locking ball and spring, elevating leg, and nut lock. Stock rest should be held firmly in bushing by ball lock.

b. Body group. - Check elevating nut for worn and damaged threads, cracks and burs. Check stem for looseness in nut and for loose pin (riveted). Check locking ball for looseness in well, and weak function with spring. Do not disassemble unless necessary, as ball is staked into stem. Check spring (if dis-assembled) for function, fracture and set, and spring well for foreign matter. Free length of spring (A152805) is 3/4 in. For

INSTRUCTIONS FOR INSPECTION TM 9-1211
54-56

removal of lock ball and spring, refer to paragraph 24 c.

c. Elevating leg group. - Check elevating screw for deformation, cracks, binding or excessive looseness in nut, worn threads, loose foot (riveted), deformed foot, and for burs. Check locking nut for looseness, wear in threads, and burs. Elevating screw and locking nut should screw without binding, but should not be so loose as to shake.

55. REAR SIGHT GROUP (M1918A2). - a. Function. - Check hinge and locking function of leaf assembly with windage screw and base spring. Check function of elevating and windage screws and click mechanism. Check zero setting of windage scale for front sight alinement. (Aline by eye.)

b. Base group. - Check rear sight base for looseness on receiver. Check dovetail and mating grooves (in receiver) for wear and burs. Check base set screw for looseness, worn threads and worn or burred nose and tool slot. Check base wings for deformation and burs. Check windage knob plunger notches and windage screw holes for wear and burs. Check windage scale for looseness on base, and screws for looseness, wear and burs. Check spring for weak function, fracture, and looseness in base.

c. Windage screw group. - Check windage screw for looseness, worn or burred threads and tool slot. Check windage knob for looseness on screw and pin for looseness in knob, and worn or burred checkering. Check click plunger for function, free movement, and worn or burred nose. Check click plunger spring for function, fracture, and set. Free length of spring (A13154) is .33 $\pm$.02 in.

d. Leaf group. - Check function of elevating screw in leaf and with slide. Check leaf and slide for deformation, wear, shine, and burs; and leaf for looseness (rock) on windage screw, and elevating screw for looseness in leaf, wear, and burs. Check click plunger for function, free movement and worn or burred nose. Check click plunger well for foreign matter. Check elevating screw knob for worn or burred checkering and click plunger notches, and for looseness on screw, and pin for looseness in knob. Check screw for missing or loose retainer pin. Check plunger spring for function, fracture, and set. Free length of spring (A163397) is .135 $\pm$.010 in.

56. REAR SIGHT GROUP (M1918 and M1918A1). - a. Function. - Check hinge function of leaf on axis screw and with base spring. Check function of elevating slide and catch. Should slide easily but not have excessive looseness.

b. Base group. - Check base for looseness on receiver.

Check dovetail and mating grooves (in receiver) for wear and burs. Check base spring screw for looseness, worn threads, and worn or burred nose and tool slot. Check base wings for deformation and burs, and axis screw holes for wear and burs.

    c. Leaf and axis screw group. - Check axis screw and nut for looseness, wear and burs. Check leaf for looseness on axis screw, wear and burs in screw tunnel, deformation, bent or burred battle aperture, aperture for shine, and foreign matter in peep hole. Check leaf for missing, loose or burred slide stop screw, and worn catch notches. Check slide for free movement on leaf, looseness, deformation, wear, and burs. Check slide aperture for shine and foreign matter in peep hole. Check slide catch for looseness on pin, loose or worn pin, worn and burred nose and serrations. Check catch spring for weak function and fracture.

    57. MAGAZINE. - a. Check magazine as a unit for binding or excessive looseness in receiver, and with catch and guides. Magazine should slide into receiver easily and catch should hold it up positively in position.

    b. Check magazine tube for dents, deformed or burred lips, and worn or burred catch lug. If lug or catch are worn sufficiently to allow magazine to drop slightly after insertion, feeding of cartridges may be affected.

    c. Check base for looseness in tube, and follower for binding in tube under spring action. Follower with spring assembled should slide smoothly up and down tube when depressed and released by a blunt instrument or cartridges. In testing, bear on entire top surface of follower, not at one point only.

    d. Check function of spring for weakness or fracture.

    e. Check magazine and parts for rust and corrosion, and interior of tube for foreign matter.

    58. INSPECTION OF GUN SLING M1907, MODIFIED. - a. Sling as a unit. - Inspect sling as a unit for appearance, general condition, flexibility, and function of hooks and sliding loops.

    b. Straps (long and short). - Check straps for condition of leather (should not crack when bent at sharp angle), weakness, ripped stitches, cuts and abrasions. Check hook holes for wear and breaks between paired holes. Check for tears at rivets, and wear and cracking at loops.

    c. Hooks and loops. - Check hooks for deformation, pinching, and burs. Check rivets for looseness. Check loops for deformation and burs. Check sliding loops for excessive looseness on straps, pinching, and burs.

    59. INSPECTION OF FRONT SIGHT COVER. - Check front sight

cover for loose retention on barrel, ease of placement and removal, deformation, dents, rust, shine, and burs.   Check hood for looseness on ring (brazed).

Section V

TOOLS FOR MAINTENANCE AND REPAIR

	Paragraph
General --	60
Special tools --	61

60. GENERAL. - The general and special tools referred to in paragraphs 30 and 31 are required in the maintenance and repair of these automatic rifles and are usually part of the equipment of an ordnance maintenance company.

61. SPECIAL TOOLS. - The special tools furnished as standard equipment for the maintenance and repair of these automatic rifles, and their uses, are as follows:

a. Tool, cleaning, gas cylinder. - This is a special tool for cleaning the gas operating mechanism. The ends of tool body may be used to scrape carbon from interior of gas cylinder and from face of gas piston. The drift attached to the body may be used to remove carbon deposits from gas ports and for grooves of gas piston. Carbon must be completely removed, but care must be exercised to avoid scoring or damaging gas cylinder walls or grooves of gas piston.

b. Tool, combination. - This tool consists of a steel body having two spanner wrenches and two screwdriver ends. Small spanner is used to turn gas cylinder and the large spanner to turn rifle barrel. Small screwdriver at the end of large spanner is used for removal of small screws, and the large screwdriver for removal of butt stock bolt (M1918 and M1918A1), butt stock retaining sleeve (M1918A2), and forearm screws.

c. Wrench, engineers. - Until a special tool is designed and issued, the 7/8 by 1 in. double head engineer's wrench may be used to remove flash hider and bipod bearing from muzzle end of rifle barrel (M1918A2).

d. Extractor, ruptured cartridge, Mk. II. - The ruptured cartridge extractor has the general form of a cal..30 cartridge. It consists of three parts: spindle, head, and sleeve. To use ruptured cartridge extractor, the live cartridges must be removed from the rifle. The ruptured cartridge extractor is then inserted through opening of ruptured cartridge case and pushed forward into the chamber. The bolt is let forward without excessive shock so extractor of the rifle engages ruptured cartridge extractor. As the operating handle is drawn back, the ruptured cartridge on its sleeve, is extracted.

Section Vl

INSTRUCTIONS FOR MAINTENANCE AND REPAIR

62. GENERAL. - <u>a</u>. The maintenance and repair of these rifles and accessories listed in this technical manual is primarily a replacement of worn or broken parts. For disassembly

and assembly of the rifle and component assemblies, refer to Section II.

   b.   Where parts, assemblies, or parts of assemblies are broken or worn so as to render them unserviceable, they must be replaced from stock. Often only parts of assemblies will be broken or worn; where it will take more time to remove the serviceable parts from the assembly than the parts are worth, the assembly should be scrapped. Parts do not always interchange and should be assembled by selection.

   c.   In general, maintenance operations are of a first aid nature, performed by qualified ordnance personnel with only the limited tool facilities afforded by repair trucks, or by semi-permanent shops at posts or camps, or by an inspector while making a regular inspection.

   63.   CROSSED THREADS, AND BURS. - a.   Crossed or burred screw threads (male or female) can be chased out by using chasing die or bottoming tap corresponding to original thread diameter and pitch.

   b.   Remove burs from screw heads with a fine file. Remove burs from cams and smooth contacting surfaces with a fine grained sharpening stone. Polish rounded surfaces with crocus cloth if necessary. · Care should be observed to stone and file evenly and lightly; do not remove too much metal. On critical surfaces, stone to polish only. Press on file or stone on forward stroke only.

   64.   BURRED, SCORED AND PROTRUDING WOOD SURFACES. - Remove burs, rough protrusions of scorings and protruding wood surfaces with a fine, flat file or fine abrasive. Always file towards an edge so as not to pick up slivers or chips. Press on file on forward stroke only. Smooth off with fine abrasive where necessary, and apply raw linseed oil.

   65.   CRACKED STOCK OR FOREARM. - If stock or forearm is cracked sufficiently to weaken it, or indicates that the crack may spread, it should be replaced. Often times, a starting crack may be checked by drilling a small hole just ahead of it. If slide grooves in forearm show superficial cracks, the section may, if not too great, be dressed out and smoothed with a sharp blade. If butt stock shows cracks near grip where buffer tube is let in, the stock should be replaced, as this is the weakest section of the stock.

   66.   DRIED-OUT WOOD OF BUTT STOCK AND FOREARM. - In dry climates, the wood of butt stock and forearm are apt to dry out and shrink. Occasional applications of raw linseed oil

will help keep wood in condition.   Apply oil to <u>wood only</u>,
allow to remain a few hours to soak in, and then wipe off and
polish with clean, dry rag.   Care should be exercised not to
allow linseed oil to get into crevices or mechanisms, as it
will "gum up" when dry.

67.   PROTRUDING WOOD SURFACES. - Where wood of butt stock
protrudes beyond butt plate or tank of receiver, it should be
filed or shaved to a flush, using fine flat file or sharp blade.

68.   WOOD SCREWS LOOSE. - If wood screws retaining butt
plate, stock rest bearing (M1918A2), or swivel bracket (M1918
and M1918A1) to butt stock become loose due to stripped threads
in wood of butt stock, they may be tightened as follows: Drill
out stripped hole with a drill about twice the major (outside)
diameter of the screw.   Fashion, from wood, a cylindrical plug
to an easy drive fit and coat with glue.   Clean out hole thoroughly and drive plug to bottom.   If plug is too tight, it will
split stock.   When glue is dry, cut plug off and file flush
with face of butt.   Then drill hole in plug with a diameter
corresponding to minor (bottom of thread) diameter of screw,
centering with prick punch, using butt plate, bearing or bracket
as a template.   Rout out threads in drilled plug if router is
available, otherwise soap screw and screw in hole to cut its
own thread.   Back screw off repeatedly to prevent thread crowd-
ing.   If screw crowds hole too much, remove screw and ream out
hole slightly.   Do not use undue force.

69.   LOOSE ESCUTCHEON IN FOREARM. - If escutcheon becomes
loose in wood of forearm and wood is "chewed up" so new seating
cannot be made, fill aperture with plastic wood, drill hole and
reseat escutcheon while plastic wood is still moist, and then
allow it to harden before tightening screw.   If plastic wood
is not available, apply glue or shellac and insert escutcheon.

70.   FOREIGN MATTER IN RIFLE MECHANISM. - Foreign matter
in mechanism of the rifle may prevent proper functioning and
should be removed.   Important parts to check are: Locking
recess in top of receiver, bolt supports, sear notch, trigger
mechanism, aperture in change lever, extractor and firing pin
wells, and sear release aperture in buffer head (M1918A2).

71.   REMOVAL OF EXCESSIVE CARBON AND RUST. - <u>a</u>. <u>Carbon</u>. -
Excessive deposits of carbon may cause malfunctioning of rifle.
Gas cylinder, piston, gas cylinder tube, and gas ports should
be cleaned as regularly as the bore of the rifle.   The gas
cylinder cleaning tool is for this purpose; for its use refer
to paragraph 61 <u>a</u>. Special care should be observed to remove

carbon thoroughly from undercut recess in gas cylinder, piston grooves, piston head, and gas ports. The relief port in gas cylinder head (M1918A2) is particularly important. The piston, gas cylinder, and gas cylinder tube should be kept clean and polished, using crocus cloth if necessary.

b. Rust. - (1) Rifle should be kept free of rust which is more apt to form on surfaces not regularly lubricated, or where barrel heat dissipates oil film rapidly. Such points are the piston shank, gas cylinder tube to rear of surface contacted by reciprocating piston, and surface where gas cylinder tube contacts bracket at barrel gas port. Rust may be removed, if light, with rifle bore cleaner and clean rag, or with fine abrasive or crocus cloth. Always wipe such surfaces with slightly oily rag, after rust is removed. To clean gas cylinder tube, use rifle cleaning rod and patches. Clean same as rifle bore. If necessary, use crocus cloth.

(2) Interior surface of actuator tube (M1918A2) should be checked for rust occasionally, and should be kept clean and polished. A .30 caliber wire rifle bore cleaning brush may be used to polish inside of tube. After cleaning, an oily patch should be passed through tube.

72. FROZEN PISTON, GAS CYLINDER OR BUFFER. - a. Frozen piston. - When piston becomes locked or "frozen" in gas cylinder, remove flash hider, and submerge barrel in kerosene until gas cylinder is covered, and soak for one hour. If this does not loosen piston, place butt stock on solid surface and with wood block, tap lightly on operating handle. Often considerable force is required to loosen piston. Clean rust and corrosion from piston, gas cylinder and tube, then polish and oil. Remove all kerosene from rifle and bore with clean rags.

b. Frozen gas cylinder. - If gas cylinder is frozen in gas cylinder tube, remove tube from rifle, clamp in vise with copper jaws, and unscrew gas cylinder with combination tool.

c. Frozen buffer. - If buffer becomes frozen in buffer tube, due to broken cups, remove operating group, trigger mechanism, and butt stock, buffer nut (M1918 and M1918A1) or cap (M1918A2), and remove buffer spring. Then soak jammed parts with kerosene and drive out from front of buffer, using hard wood plug. If parts do not dislodge easily, remove buffer tube from receiver, and place on hard wood block and drive out parts as above. If cups and cones are frozen together, soak in kerosene and tap edge of cup until loose. Clean parts thoroughly, test, oil, and replace. Reassemble rifle.

73. WEAK EJECTION. - Weak ejection of cartridge case may be caused by neck of ejector scraping on bolt, neck bent or too short, or nose worn. To correct, grind nose off, being careful to maintain angle, straighten or replace ejector. Space between ejector and bolt should not be more than 1/32 in.

74. UNCONTROLLED AUTOMATIC FIRE WITH CHANGE LEVER SET AT "F". - May be due to: a. Clogged gas ports. - Clogged gas ports may cause weak functioning of operating mechanism, preventing slide from traveling far enough to rear to engage sear. Clean out all ports. If this does not correct trouble, switch to next larger control port.

b. Foreign matter on face of buffer or rear end of slide. - Blown primer or other foreign matter on face of buffer, or rear end of slide may cause same malfunction as clogged gas ports. Clean buffer face, or rear end of slide.

75. FAILURE OF RIFLE TO PULL OFF WITH CHANGE LEVER SET AT "F", OR "A", WITH MUZZLE DEPRESSED. - Usually caused by incorrect positioning of deformation of outside prongs of sear spring, so that they are not resting squarely on forward shoulders of sear and center prong is not properly contacting connector. Position spring correctly or bend prongs until contact is correct, or replace spring.

76. FRONT SIGHT BLADE OUT OF ALINEMENT. - This is usually due to enlarged dovetail aperture in base. Peen lightly along upper edges and realine sight blade (by eye) using old stake mark and restake. Base pin may be missing; if so, replace and aline blade.

77. REPLACING UNSERVICEABLE BARREL. - a. To replace unserviceable barrel, disassemble rifle and remove barrel as explained in paragraph 18.

b. Assemble new barrel assembly, which includes front sight base and gas cylinder tube bracket. Screw up barrel until draw marks on barrel and receiver register. Assemble gas cylinder tube to bracket, then check fit and alinement of rear tang and retaining pin holes in tang and receiver. If tang of tube will not mate without binding, turn barrel until this is accomplished. Barrel should draw up tightly to receiver so there is no possibility of vibrating loose. Use qualifying shim if necessary, either made from thin sheet brass or procured from Springfield Arsenal. If there is no draw mark on barrel, draw up until tube alines as above, and check position of extractor cut by assembling bolt with extractor assembled.

c. If barrel will not draw up to proper position, dress

off rear face of shoulder in a lathe, or, in case of necessity, with a fine file with safe edge. If barrel draws <u>by</u> draw mark and no shim is available, rear shoulder of barrel may be peened lightly to a fit. This practice is not advised.

<u>d</u>. Never alter the receiver to obtain draw fit. When barrel is alined, check alinement of gas cylinder tube, front sight, and extractor cut. If barrel requires much shimming or dressing to aline, headspace may be affected.

78. CORRECTIONS FOR EXCESSIVE HEADSPACE. - <u>a</u>. When the headspace is found to be excessive (refer to par. 48) due to worn bolt, bolt lock, or receiver, it may be corrected in the field by selective replacement of bolt assemblies. New bolt may often be fitted to old bolt lock, or vice versa, to form a serviceable bolt assembly by selection of maximum components. To ascertain this, disassemble bolt assembly by punching out bolt lock pin. Assemble bolts and bolt locks selectively until combination is found that will produce the correct headspace. In order to salvage receivers with worn locking shoulders and those manufactured to maximum tolerances, a quantity of bolt locks were manufactured to take an adjusting plate. These bolt locks with the adjusting plate are only for use at arsenals and will not be issued to the field.

<u>b</u>. When headspace is found to be excessive, due to excessive depth of chamber, barrel should be replaced. Refer to paragraph 47 <u>c</u> (2) (<u>g</u>).

<u>c</u>. When headspace is found to be excessive due to worn locking chamber in receiver, the rifle should be sent to an arsenal for overhaul.

79. ROUGH OR WAVY SURFACE OF BOLT LOCKING RECESS IN RECEIVER. - If surface of bolt locking recess in receiver is burred or <u>wavy</u>, it can be corrected by removing trigger and operating mechanism from the receiver and driving top plate out to front, using block of hard wood, and stoning rough or wavy surface smooth with a fine sharpening stone. Care must be used to stone evenly and remove as little metal as possible, as this surface affects headspace. Check headspace after stoning.

80. GAS CYLINDER TUBE OUT OF LINE WITH RECEIVER. - If gas cylinder tube is out of line with receiver, it may be caused by one of several factors; deformed tube, missing tube bracket retaining pin (affecting positioning of bracket), or barrel improperly assembled to receiver. To correct; straighten tube, replace pin and/or reposition barrel with receiver. Test function of slide and piston with tube after repairs.

NOTE: The gas cylinder tube bracket pin hole is drilled at manufacture after the barrel is alined to receiver, with respect to extractor cut, to insure alinement of gas cylinder tube bracket and tube with receiver, together with extractor cut, and front sight base. This fact should be taken into consideration when assembling new parts.

81. ALINEMENT OF PISTON AND SLIDE. - The piston and slide are assembled to a loose fit at manufacture. The piston is screwed in slide and then backed off sufficiently to allow some play in union, slide and piston are then tested for free sliding fit in receiver and gas cylinder tube; if satisfactory, pin hole is drilled and pin assembled. In assembling new piston or slide, this practice should be followed. Test freedom of sliding movement by tilting rifle.

82. DEFORMED SIDE RAILS OF SLIDE. - Side rails of slide may become bent in or out, causing binding with operating mechanism or receiver. Rails can be spread or sprung in by using wooden wedges or clamping in vise with copper jaws, or with hands. Test slide after repair for free sliding movement by tilting rifle.

83. LOOSE SPRING ON GAS CYLINDER TUBE RETAINING PIN. - If spring becomes loose from body of pin, it may be impossible to withdraw pin by ordinary methods, for replacement. In such a case, first attempt to revolve and shake pin out of aperture or pull out with needle nosed pliers. If this fails, drive pin from left to right with a punch until nose of key is sheared off by receiver, and then punch it out of left side of receiver. Correct locking shoulder in receiver if damaged, and replace damaged pin with new one.

84. OPERATING HANDLE ASSEMBLED INCORRECTLY. - The operating handle is provided with a small projection on rear end to prevent incorrect assembly. If, however, this projection is missing, it is possible to assemble handle to the receiver incorrectly with knob to the rear. If so assembled, it will be impossible to aline hole in handle with hammer pin, preventing punching out of pin and subsequent withdrawal of operating handle from receiver. If pin will not shake out, locate point on handle coincident with position of firing pin when registered with its insertion aperture on right side of receiver, drill a hole in handle large enough to insert a punch, register firing pin with aperture, and punch out hammer pin. Handle can then be withdrawn and assembled correctly.

85. LOOSE RIVETS IN BOLT SUPPORTS. - If bolt support

rivets become loose, they may be tightened by expanding body of
rivet with a heavy hammer. Disassemble rifle and position receiver on solid metal support, such as an "L" of heavy iron
clamped in vise, or wedge an iron block in receiver so that
bearing on bolt support and rivet will be level; protect oppo-
site side of receiver with wood block; then strike rivet with
ball headed hammer, being careful to strike rivet only and not
receiver. Hammer should be heavy enough to expand body of rivet
and not merely peen down head, which will quickly wear loose
again. Stone both ends of rivet flush and smooth. Where possible, rifle should be completely disassembled, including removal
of barrel and receiver, and body reparkerized. If rivets are
badly worn, replace.

86. DENTS IN BUFFER, ACTUATOR AND GAS CYLINDER TUBES. -
Shallow dents in buffer, actuator or gas cylinder tube may often
be removed by reaming with an expansion reamer, set to original
inside diameter of tube. Larger dents may be swedged out first,
by using iron rod the size of inside diameter of tube, and then
reaming. If dents are deep enough to cause possible weakening
of wall of tube due to this procedure, the tube should be replaced. This is particularly important in the case of the gas
cylinder tube. Test components in tubes after repairs, for
free movement.

87. FITTING NEW TRIGGER GUARD, GAS CYLINDER TUBE OR STOCK. -
a. In fitting new trigger guard to receiver, it may be found
that trigger guard retaining pin holes in trigger guard body and
receiver are not concentric. In such a case, stone off rear
beveled surface of trigger guard or mating lug on receiver
slightly to aline holes. Use fine grained sharpening stone.

b. In fitting new gas cylinder tube to receiver, it may
be found that pin holes in tang of tube and receiver are not
concentric. In such a case, stone rear tang on gas cylinder
tube to fit, using fine grained sharpening stone. Be sure tube
is properly alined before attempting to fit. Refer to paragraph
80.

c. When fitting new stock to receiver, dress stock to a
close fit with receiver, using fine file and/or sharp blade.

88. STONING NOSE OF SEAR. - If nose of sear or sear notch
in slide becomes worn or burred, it may be stoned lightly with
a fine sharpening stone. Care must be taken to maintain retentive angle, and stone to polish only. If too much metal is
removed from top of face of the M1918A2 sear, the face will become too shallow to retain slide, due to interference of rear

end of sear (release cam extension) with the slide, thus holding sear notch out of engagement. Test sear retentive action after stoning, and if found questionable, replace sear. Notch in slide may be dressed in like manner.

89. MAINTENANCE AND REPAIR OF GUN SLING, M1907, MODIFIED. - a. Dried out (dead) leather. - When straps become stiff or dried out (indicated by light cracking), a thorough dressing with castile or saddle soap will help condition the leather. A thick lather of soap should be well worked into the leather and allowed to remain for a half hour; then rub off residue and polish briskly with dry, clean rag.

b. Scratches and gouges. - When straps become rough from leather "picked up" by scratches, cuts or gouges they may be smoothed by paring lightly with a sharp thin blade.

c. Bent sliding loops and hooks. - When sliding loops or hooks become spread or pinched they should be corrected. Loops may be spread by placing a piece of flat metal between loop and strap, then tapping with a light hammer. Spread loops or hooks may be hammered into shape.

d. Worn holes in straps. - When paired holes in straps become worn or leather is torn between holes, the strap should be replaced. Punching new holes will weaken strap.

90. MAINTENANCE AND REPAIR OF FRONT SIGHT COVER. - a. Deformed hood or ring. - (1) If hood of front sight cover becomes deformed or dented, it may be straightened by inserting piece of round or flat iron in opening and, holding on vise or similar firm metal base, striking with light hammer at points necessary to remove dents or deformations.

(2) Deformed ring can be repaired in similar manner, or laid on anvil of vise and hammered flat.

b. Cracked welding. - Ring is welded to hood. If welding becomes cracked, it can be repaired by tack welding at point of rupture.

c. Rust. - Remove rust with rifle bore cleaner or oil on clean rag. Abrasive will cause "shine" on sight cover.

91. CLEANING AND LUBRICATION. - a. Bore. - Assemble a cloth patch to the cleaning rod, saturate with CLEANER, rifle bore, and insert into the muzzle end of the bore. Move it back and forth several times and replace with a new patch, repeating the operation until the patch comes out clean. In cleaning the bore, take care not to foul the cleaning patch in the gas port. If CLEANER, rifle bore, is not available, water may be used; in this case, it is necessary that the bore be dried thoroughly

afterward. Inspect the bore for metal fouling. Remove any
which may be found according to instructions in TM 9-850. To
lubricate, saturate a patch with oil and push it through the
bore.

b. Internal parts. - Clean all internal metal surfaces
with a clean, dry cloth to remove moisture, perspiration and
dirt. Then wipe with a cloth containing a small quantity of
oil. Maintain this protective film at all times, using the oil
designated in subparagraph f below.

c. Chamber. - Place the cleaning patch on the chamber
cleaning tool and insert the tool into the chamber. Twist the
patch-covered tool in the chamber to insure thorough cleaning
of its entire length.

d. Gas cylinder and gas cylinder plug. - Carbon will
accumulate in the gas cylinder due to firing. Frequency of
carbon removal is a factor peculiar to the individual rifle.
Scrape the carbon from the cylinder and plug with a sharp bladed
instrument. If an abrasive cloth is used, take care that the
corners of the plug or piston head are not rounded. Clean the
cylinder with a rod and patch.

e. Exterior surfaces. - Wipe the exterior of the rifle
with a dry cloth to remove dampness, dirt, and perspiration.
Wipe all metal surfaces with a slightly oiled cloth. Oil the
stock with OIL, linseed, raw, and oil the sling with OIL, neat's-
foot.

f. Lubricating oils. - The lubricants to be used are:

OIL, lubricating, for aircraft instruments and machine
guns (between 0° F and 45° F).
OIL, sperm (above 45° F).
OIL, engine, SAE 10 (if OIL, sperm is not available).

g. Care in arctic climate. - Clean all parts with dry
cloths and lubricate only the parts that show wear with OIL,
lubricating, for aircraft instruments and machine guns. When
cold rifles are placed in a warm room, wipe them frequently with
dry cloths to remove condensed moisture. If necessary, heat the
OIL, neat's-foot before applying it to the sling. Do not boil.

92. PREPARING RIFLES FOR STORAGE. - Rifles should be
cleaned and prepared with particular care. The bore, all parts
of the mechanism, and the exterior of the rifles should be
cleaned thoroughly and then dried with rags until absolutely no
moisture is left on the metal. After drying a part, do not
touch it with the bare hands. Special care should be taken to

insure that the gas system is thoroughly clean and that the gas ports are free from fouling. Coat all metal parts heavily with rust-preventive compound. Handling the rifle by the stock and forearm only, place it in the packing chest after painting the wooden supports at the butt and muzzle with rust-preventive compound. A rifle in a cloth or other cover, or with a plug in the bore, should not be placed in storage, as such articles collect moisture, which causes the weapon to rust.

93. CLEANING RIFLES RECEIVED FROM STORAGE. - Rifles received from storage are coated completely with rust-preventive compound. Use SOLVENT, dry-cleaning, to remove all traces of this compound, taking particular care that the gas system gas ports, firing pin, and all recesses in which springs or plungers operate are cleaned thoroughly. After using the SOLVENT, dry-cleaning, make sure it is completely removed from all parts by wiping with light-colored cloths until no staining of the cloth occurs. Bore and chamber of the barrel must be cleaned thoroughly. All surfaces having been thoroughly cleaned, they should then be protected with a thin film of OIL, lubricating, applied with a rag.

Section VII

References

	Paragraph
Standard nomenclature lists	94
Explanatory publications	95

94. STANDARD NOMENCLATURE LISTS. -

a. Ammunition, rifle and automatic gun ------- SNL T-1

b. Cleaning and preserving. -

Cleaning, preserving and lubricating materials, recoil fluids, special oils, and similar items of issue	SNL K-1
Soldering, brazing, and welding materials	SNK K-2

c. Gun materiel. -

Rifle, automatic, cal..30, Browning, M1918	SNL A-4
Tools, special repair, automatic guns, automatic gun antiaircraft materiel, automatic and semiautomatic cannon, and mortars	SNL A-35
Trucks, small arms, repair, M1	SNL G-72
Current Standard Nomenclature Lists are as tabulated here. An up-to-date list of SNL's is maintained as the "Ordnance Publications for Supply Index"	OPSI

95. EXPLANATORY PUBLICATIONS. -

a. Ammunition, general ----------------------- TM 9-1900

b. Cleaning, preserving, lubricating, and

welding materials and similar items issued by the Ordnance Department	TM 9-850

c. Gun Materiel. -

Browning automatic rifle, cal..30, M1918A2, with bipod	FM 23-15
Browning automatic rifle, cal..30, M1918, without bipod	FM 23-20
Defense against chemical attack	FM 21-40
Ordnance maintenance procedure - Materiel inspection and repair	TM 9-1100

(Numbers in parentheses refer to paragraphs)

Page

A

Page

(A. G. 062.11 (12-13-41) PC-C.)

BY ORDER OF THE SECRETARY OF WAR:

G. C. MARSHALL,
Chief of Staff.

OFFICIAL:

  E. S. ADAMS,
    Major General,
    The Adjutant General.

DISTRIBUTION: IBn 9(2); IC 9(4)